Contents

WORDLY WISE 3000®

SECOND EDITION

Book **10**

Kenneth Hodkinson | Sandra Adams

EDUCATORS PUBLISHING SERVICE
Cambridge and Toronto

Original cover design: Hugh Price
Interior design: Sarah Cole
Acquisitions/Development: Kate Moltz
Editors: Wendy Drexler, Elissa Gershowitz, Stacey Nichols Kim, Theresa Trinder, Laura Woollett
Editorial Assistant: Becky Ticotsky
Senior Editorial Manager: Sheila Neylon

Printed in the U.S.A.

978-0-8388-2828-1

3 4 5 6 7 CUR 11 10 09 08 07

Lesson 1

Word List
Study the definitions of the words below; then do the exercises for the lesson.

asperity
ə sper´ ə tē

n. 1. Sharpness or harshness of manner.
There was a noticeable **asperity** in her voice as she scolded the children for teasing Andrea.
2. Roughness of surface; unevenness.
Running my fingers over the new countertop, I detected a certain **asperity**.

bane
bān

n. A person or thing that destroys or causes harm.
Jonathan's little brother was the **bane** of our slumber party.
baneful *adj.* Causing destruction or ruin.
Hitler's **baneful** rule ended with his death in 1945.

buffoon
bə foon´

n. A person who often makes attempts to be funny; a clown; a fool.
Although he acted like a **buffoon** at parties, Matt was usually rather serious.

doleful
dōl´ fəl

adj. Mournful or full of sorrow; causing grief.
The **doleful** look on her face told me she had not gotten the grant to go to the summer program.

extrovert
eks´ trə vurt

n. A person whose attention is focused on others and on what is going on around her or him, rather than on her or his own feelings.
Ray is an **extrovert** now, but he was rather shy as a young child.
extroverted *adj.*
Because she is so **extroverted**, she loves to perform in front of a large crowd.

garish
gâr´ ish

adj. Excessively bright and flashy; tastelessly glaring.
I told Henry that his tie was too **garish** to wear to a job interview.

hierarchy
hī´ ər är kē

n. A group or system in which positions of power are ranked, usually from lowest to highest.
In the state government **hierarchy**, the governor is at the top.

imbue
im byōō´

v. To fill completely with a feeling or idea; to inspire.
The really great athletes are **imbued** with a desire to excel.

instigate
in´ stə gāt

v. To stir up or urge on; to provoke.
Because Joy was jealous of Dara's friendship with Kim, she **instigated** an argument between them.

penchant
pen´ chənt

n. A strong attraction or leaning.
Susan and Carl shared a **penchant** for crossword puzzles and made a ritual of doing them together every Sunday morning.

rambunctious
ram buŋk´ shəs

adj. Behaving in a wild and unruly manner.
When the puppies get too **rambunctious** in their play, the trainer separates them.

repertoire
rep´ ər twär

n. The list of pieces an actor, musician, etc., is ready to perform; the skills or accomplishments of a person or group.
The band knew most of the requests, but several songs were not part of its **repertoire**.

rudiment
roo˝ də mənt

n. (usually plural) 1. A basic principle or skill.
This book teaches the **rudiments** of cooking, but it will not make you a master chef.
2. An undeveloped or beginning stage.
The **rudiments** of the club's plan to raise money seemed promising until we discussed them more, at which point we realized how unrealistic they were.

undermine
un´ dər mīn

v. 1. To weaken or ruin by degrees.
His smoking habit seriously **undermined** his health.
2. To attack by indirect, secret, or underhanded means.
During World War II, the French underground sought to **undermine** the Nazi occupation.

unremitting
un rē mit´ iŋ

adj. Not stopping or slowing down; constant.
The **unremitting** sounds of the city kept me awake in my hotel room all night.

1A Understanding Meanings

Read the sentences below. If a sentence correctly uses the word in bold, write *C* on the line below it. If a sentence is incorrect, rewrite it so that the vocabulary word in bold is used correctly.

1. A **doleful** tale is one that expresses sadness or gloom.

C

2. A **penchant** is a fondness for something.

James held a penchant for lacrosse.

3. One's **repertoire** is one's range of skills or accomplishments.

C

asperity
bane
buffoon
doleful
extrovert
garish
hierarchy
imbue
instigate
penchant
rambunctious
repertoire
rudiment
undermine
unremitting

4. An **unremitting** effort is one made in a halfhearted manner.

5. **Asperity** is abrasive behavior.

6. A **rambunctious** crowd is one that is excessively exuberant.

7. **Rudiments** are basic skills.

8. A **buffoon** is a person who tries to amuse people with tricks and silliness.

_____

9. A **hierarchy** is a group that is organized according to status.

_____

10. To **undermine** a plan is to work subtly to make sure that it isn't executed.

_____

11. An **extrovert** is an effort that goes beyond what is expected.

_____

12. To be **imbued** with a quality is to have it in abundance.

_____

13. To **instigate** something is to examine it closely.

_____

14. A **garish** display is one that is showy to the point of gaudiness.

_____

15. A **baneful** policy is one that is full of hate.

_____

1B Using Words

If the word (or a form of the word) in bold fits in a sentence in the group below it, write the word in the blank. If the word does not fit, leave the space empty.

1. **garish**

   (a) Walter gave me a _____ look when I mistook his wife for his daughter.

   (b) The school gym was covered with _____ decorations for the dance.

   (c) The multicolored sequined dress was a little too _____ for my taste.

2. penchant

(a) Trina's _____ for long words sometimes makes her sound pretentious.

(b) Isolation from the company of others had made him increasingly _____ .

(c) A _____ for stretching the truth gave Jamie a reputation for being unreliable.

3. buffoon

(a) With his ill-fitting suit and mismatched socks, he looked like a _____ .

(b) The salesperson tried to _____ us into paying twice what the watch was worth.

(c) Whenever Angela tried to _____ her brother, he got annoyed and walked away.

4. bane

(a) Our neighbors caused us so much _____ we were forced to move.

(b) Mosquitoes are the _____ of people camping in the northern woods this season.

(c) The _____ effects of DDT led to the banning of this toxic pesticide in the United States.

5. repertoire

(a) The magician's _____ included making rabbits disappear into thin air.

(b) The 1929 Bentley was the prize object in the antique car collector's _____ .

(c) Kevin demonstrated for us his incredible _____ of bird calls.

6. undermine

(a) Your constant criticism will seriously _____ his confidence in his ability.

(b) Reports of mismanagement _____ the public's confidence in the agency.

(c) Interfering with her practice sessions will _____ her chances of winning the cello competition.

7. instigate

(a) A mutiny doesn't start by itself; someone has to _____ it.

(b) The amateur detective vowed to _____ the dreadful crime.

(c) The college will _____ its new admissions policy immediately.

8. imbue

(a) The stump was so deeply _____ in the ground that we couldn't remove it.

(b) All their children were _____ with a deep love of learning.

(c) She _____ in her followers a deep loyalty to her beliefs.

asperity
bane
buffoon
doleful
extrovert
garish
hierarchy
imbue
instigate
penchant
rambunctious
repertoire
rudiment
undermine
unremitting

1C Word Study

Each group of four words below contains two words that are either synonyms or antonyms. Circle these two words; then circle the *S* if they are synonyms, the *A* if they are antonyms.

1. baneful   ecstatic   doleful   questionable   S   A

2. fill   instigate   recall   imbue   S   A

3. hierarchy   penchant   aversion   description   S   A

4. roughness   instigation   clarity   asperity   S   A

5. docile   garish   rambunctious   clever   S   A

6. garish   unremitting   thoughtful   plain   S   A

7. provoke   undermine   instigate   overlook   S   A

8. undermine   support   begin   barter   S   A

9. constant   silent   baneful   unremitting   S   A

10. blessing   hierarchy   bane   buffoon   S   A

1D Images of Words

Circle the letter of each sentence that suggests the numbered bold vocabulary word. In each group, you may circle more than one letter or none at all.

1. **extroverted**

   (a) No matter what I say, you seem to take pleasure in disagreeing with me.

   (b) I notice that Sandy spends more and more time alone in her room.

   (c) Ever since he was a child, James has liked to take part in all group activities.

2. **asperity**

   (a) "Don't you dare contradict me," she said to her son.

   (b) The engine knocks loudly because it needs a tune-up.

   (c) Wearing coarse wool next to sensitive skin can cause a rash.

3. **unremitting**

   (a) My grandparents worked for twelve months on the house and never took a day off.

   (b) The Eagles kept up the pressure on the Colts for the entire game.

   (c) After thirty days, the drought showed no signs of ending any time soon.

4. **rambunctious**

    (a) Lucy was disappointed with the ending to the novel.

    (b) The garden had been sadly neglected and was overgrown with weeds.

    (c) Joan's orange coat clashed horribly with her pink pants.

5. **hierarchy**

    (a) The Arc de Triomphe, a central landmark in Paris, was completed in 1835.

    (b) The captain let me see the major, who then allowed me to see the colonel.

    (c) In chess, a queen is a more powerful piece than either a rook or a knight.

6. **doleful**

    (a) The headline read, "Earthquake Fatalities Exceed 2,000."

    (b) The song was about the Great Famine that devastated Ireland.

    (c) I could tell by their expressions that the rescue mission had failed.

7. **instigate**

    (a) The server suggested that we try the goulash, which she said was delicious.

    (b) The starter fired the pistol, and the 400-meter relay got underway.

    (c) "Something is not right here, and I intend to get to the bottom of it," said Hector.

8. **rudiments**

    (a) For his first basketball lesson, I taught Jon how to dribble the ball.

    (b) My grandmother commented on my impolite behavior.

    (c) Coach Ginsberg was surprised by how quickly I learned the basic moves.

9. **undermine**

    (a) Another big storm could collapse that wall.

    (b) Maura's hiking boots were so worn-out that they couldn't be repaired.

    (c) Termites had weakened the beams on which the floor rested.

10. **repertoire**

    (a) Abbot and Costello exchanged impromptu quips that had the audience in fits of laughter.

    (b) The band plans to add two new songs to its Friday night performance.

    (c) Bonnie plays six instruments and is proficient on all of them.

asperity
bane
buffoon
doleful
extrovert
garish
hierarchy
imbue
instigate
penchant
rambunctious
repertoire
rudiment
undermine
unremitting

1E Passage

Read the passage below; then complete the exercise that follows it.

Clown College

When Irvin Feld purchased Ringling Brothers Barnum & Bailey Circus in 1967, he was concerned that the number of clowns in his circus was dwindling. The circus had only about a dozen clowns and the average age of the group was about sixty. After seeing some clowns perform, Feld remarked with **asperity**, "They can fall down, but can they get up?"

Feld found a solution to his problem in 1968 when he started a school that would train a new generation of clowns. It ran for thirty years and at its peak was receiving thousands of applications from those **imbued** with a desire to make people laugh. During their audition, applicants might be asked to walk like a lizard or to pretend they're on a planet with too much gravity and then on one with too little. Only about thirty were accepted each year, usually the most **extroverted**. Shyness had to be overcome or it would **undermine** their chances of success. The college's director once said what he looked for in a clown was "a heart as big as Alaska and [a willingness] to give it away on a daily basis."

After admission, eight weeks of **unremitting** hard work faced the successful applicants. For fourteen hours a day, six days a week, students learned the **rudiments** of clowning. Classes were typically taught by veteran clowns, many of whom were big-name circus performers at the top of the circus **hierarchy**. Their day began with warm-ups at 8:00 a.m., followed by an hour-long makeup class. From 9:30 a.m. until dinnertime, students practiced the physical aspects of clowning: tumbling, taking pratfalls, walking on stilts, riding unicycles, and juggling. At the same time, they worked on developing their own **repertoire** of tricks and stunts. They also had to decide which of the two basic types of clown they aspired to be.

The auguste (pronounced *oh-GOOST*) wears **garish** clothing several sizes too big for him or her. The makeup is greatly exaggerated, and the costume often features a bright red fake nose and curly orange wig. The **bane** of the other clowns, the auguste specializes in **rambunctious** behavior and delights in **instigating** mischief in the circus ring and acting like a **buffoon**. Hampered by a pair of enormous shoes, the auguste is often seen being chased around the ring by an authority figure like a police officer or the ringmaster.

Students with a **penchant** for mime are often drawn to the other basic type, known as the whiteface clown. Makeup for the whiteface is applied sparingly around the eyes and mouth, over a white base. The shoes are a normal size and the costume is loose-fitting. The hair is completely hidden under a skullcap, over which the whiteface wears a neat, cone-shaped hat. Much of circus comedy is based on interactions between the auguste and the whiteface clowns. The whiteface is often a victim of the auguste's antics and therefore usually has a **doleful** expression.

In 1995 Clown College moved from Florida to Wisconsin, and two years later, as a result of cost-cutting measures, it closed its doors permanently. During its thirty years it graduated about fifteen hundred clowns. Class reunions are held every year when about three hundred present and former clowns get together to swap stories of circus life. With no more clowns being graduated, many of them tell of receiving calls from the circus, inviting them to return. But the work is hard, the pay is low, and the turnover is high. Not many are tempted by such offers. All agree, however, that their experience with the circus was an exciting time of their lives. They had lived a childhood dream: they ran away to join the circus.

Answer each of the following questions in the form of a sentence. If a question does not contain a vocabulary word from this lesson's word list, use one in your answer. Use each word only once.

1. How did Feld express his opinion of the state of the clowns in his circus in 1967?

2. What kind of person is likely to apply to Clown College?

3. Why would shyness **undermine** an audition to Clown College?

4. Is Clown College all fun and games?

5. What do students learn at Clown College?

6. Why might one conclude that students at Clown College get a good education in clowning?

7. What kind of student might be interested in becoming a whiteface clown?

8. How does the auguste's makeup and hair differ from those of the whiteface clown?

9. How would you characterize the auguste?

10. Why is the auguste the **bane** of the other clowns?

FUN & FASCINATING FACTS

The Latin *dolere* means "to feel pain." This word is the root of several English words that refer to suffering. A life of *dolor* is one filled with sorrow. To wear a **doleful** expression is to look unhappy. *Indolent* once meant "free of pain" but changed its meaning over time and now means "lazy" or "avoiding exertion."

Extrovert and its antonym *introvert* are formed from the Latin verb *vertere*, "to turn," combined with the prefixes *extro-*, "outward," and *intro-*, "within," respectively. Extroverts are people who turn their attention to what is going on outside themselves; introverts are people who turn their attention inward, focusing on their own feelings and thoughts.

Repertoire and *repertory* can be used interchangeably in some instances. One can speak of a singer's *repertoire* of songs or of a singer's *repertory* of songs. However, in this case, *repertoire* is the preferred term. *Repertory* is also the term for a type of theatrical practice in which several different plays are put on in rotation over the course of a season. Many actors learn their skills in repertory. A repertory company may put on a tragedy one night and a comedy the next, with the same actors performing in both plays.

Lesson 2

Word List
Study the definitions of the words below; then do the exercises for the lesson.

adjudicate
ə jōōd´ i kāt
v. To hear and decide judicially; to judge.
Since her case was still being **adjudicated**, the defendant didn't want to speak to the press.
adjudicator *n.*
Anne is trained as an **adjudicator** in marital disputes.

centennial
sen ten´ ē əl
n. A one-hundredth anniversary or its celebration.
The nation celebrated its **centennial** in 1876, one hundred years after the Declaration of Independence was adopted on July 4, 1776.
adj. Of or pertaining to a period of one hundred years.
A **centennial** fair celebrated the town's one-hundredth birthday.

countenance
koun´ tə nəns
n. 1. A person's face; the expression on a person's face.
Luke's **countenance** was doleful when he heard the news that the class trip was cancelled.
2. Support or approval.
The measure to abolish bilingual education cannot pass without the party leaders' **countenance**.
v. To support or approve; to tolerate.
The school board will not **countenance** a shorter school day.

disgruntle
dis grunt´ l
v. To make dissatisfied; to put in a bad mood.
The employees, who haven't been given a raise in over two years, are **disgruntled** with their wages and want an increase in pay.

equilibrium
ē kwi lib´ rē əm
n. A state of balance.
The United States government is most effective when its executive, legislative, and judicial branches are all working in **equilibrium**.

expedite
ek´ spə dīt
v. To speed up a process; to facilitate.
The company hired additional workers to **expedite** the delivery of holiday orders.
expeditious *adj.* With great speed; quick and efficient.
Because we were catering two parties back-to-back, we had to work in an **expeditious** manner.

gird
gʉrd
v. 1. To encircle, bind, or surround.
He **girded** his waist with a wide leather belt.
2. To get ready for action; to brace.
As 1941 drew to a close, America **girded** itself for a war of unremitting ferocity.

gratuitous
grə tōō´ ət əs
adj. 1. Not called for; unnecessary.
The violence in that movie was **gratuitous** because it didn't add to the plot.
2. Without charge; free.
Did you think the skating lessons would be **gratuitous**, or did you expect to pay for them?

illusory
il lōō´ sər ē
adj. Unreal or imagined; deceiving.
His chances of getting a raise were **illusory** since he had such a poor work record.

implacable im plak´ ə bəl	*adj.* Incapable of being placated, soothed, or significantly changed; relentless. Despite Gina's apologies, Karen still felt hurt by her friend's betrayal and remained **implacable**.
luminary loo´ mə ner ē	*n.* 1. A source of light, especially from the sky, such as the sun or moon. The moon far outshines all other **luminaries** in the night sky. 2. A person who is well known for her or his achievements; a celebrity. The Academy Awards presentations were attended by many Hollywood **luminaries**.
manifesto man ə fes´ tō	*n.* A public statement explaining the intentions, motives, or views of an individual or group. In their 1848 Communist **Manifesto**, Karl Marx and Friedrich Engels outlined their philosophies about class and economics.
mesmerize mez´ mər īz	*v.* To fascinate or hypnotize. The agile, death-defying moves of the trapeze artist kept the audience **mesmerized** during her performance.
precedent pres´ ə dənt	*n.* An act or statement that may serve as an example or justification for a later one. The successful revolt of the American colonies provided **a precedent** for the French Revolution.
spurious spyoor´ ē əs	*adj.* Not genuine; false. **Spurious** reports that Elvis Presley was alive kept appearing in the tabloids.

2A Understanding Meanings

Read the sentences below. If a sentence correctly uses the word in bold, write *C* on the line below it. If a sentence is incorrect, rewrite it so that the vocabulary word in bold is used correctly.

1. A **centennial** is a person who is celebrating a one-hundredth birthday.

_____

2. An **implacable** course of action is one that can't be significantly modified.

_____

3. People who are **disgruntled** feel they have something to complain about.

_____

4. To **countenance** a suggestion is to show approval of it.

_____

5. A **luminary** is someone who is well known.

_____

6. To **mesmerize** someone is to have a distinct memory of that person.

7. **Equilibrium** is a state of unrest.

8. An **illusory** goal is one that cannot be attained.

9. A **gratuitous** service is one that is not paid for.

10. A **precedent** is something that is used as a model for subsequent actions.

11. To **adjudicate** is to make a decision concerning an issue.

12. A **manifesto** is a list of items required for proper record keeping.

13. A **spurious** claim is one that is fraudulent.

14. To **gird** a tree is to put something around it.

15. To **expedite** a process is to help to advance it.

adjudicate
centennial
countenance
disgruntle
equilibrium
expedite
gird
gratuitous
illusory
implacable
luminary
manifesto
mesmerize
precedent
spurious

2B Using Words

If the word (or a form of the word) in bold fits in a sentence in the group below it, write the word in the blank. If the word does not fit, leave the space empty.

1. **gratuitous**

   (a) The food provided at the church was _____ and available to all travelers.

   (b) Telling Kate she looked skinny was a _____ insult that hurt her deeply.

   (c) "I'm very _____ to you for your kind assistance," she said warmly.

2. **precedent**

   (a) We searched the law books trying to find a _____ for the judge's action.

   (b) Oysters on the half shell were the _____ for the main course.

   (c) Britain created a _____ when it elected its first female prime minister.

3. **countenance**

   (a) Why does he _____ such disrespectful behavior from his students?

   (b) He had a _____ that expressed both good humor and intelligence.

   (c) The _____ of votes cast showed an almost 90 percent turnout.

4. **gird**

   (a) Congress _____ itself for a tough battle with the president over tax cuts.

   (b) A metal band _____ the structure, giving it added strength.

   (c) We believe we were _____ through those trying times by our convictions.

5. **adjudicate**

   (a) Alida and Mike called upon the camp counselor to _____ the dispute between them.

   (b) The federal courts _____ cases concerning immigration to the United States.

   (c) Yvette felt that she had an _____ reason for refuting the case.

6. **mesmerize**

   (a) The winking light _____ me, and I could not turn my head away from it.

   (b) Antonio had _____ his entire speech and had no need to refer to his notes.

   (c) Even small babies are _____ by the flickering images on the television screen.

7. **luminary**

   (a) Laurence Olivier was a _____ of the stage for over five decades.

   (b) Some of the _____ that we see in the night sky are distant stars.

   (c) Zack had a _____ idea at the meeting last Friday.

8. **equilibrium**

(a) The system is stable when all the forces acting on it are in _____ .

(b) Despite being pulled in various directions, she maintained her _____ .

(c) A finely balanced _____ is used to measure small quantities accurately.

2C Word Study

Complete the analogies by selecting the pair of words whose relationship most resembles the relationship of the pair in capital letters. Circle the letter in front of the pair you choose.

1. DISGRUNTLED : COMPLAIN ::
   (a) pleased : praise
   (b) implacable : surrender
   (c) illusory : pretend
   (d) lost : return

2. IMPLACABLE : YIELD ::
   (a) gratuitous : forgive
   (b) talkative : chat
   (c) unremitting : stop
   (d) friendly : smile

3. MESMERIZE : BORE ::
   (a) imbue : empty
   (b) undermine : betray
   (c) gird : brace
   (d) instigate : provoke

4. COUNTENANCE : UNDERMINE ::
   (a) respond : reply
   (b) adjudicate : judge
   (c) respect : praise
   (d) expedite : delay

5. ASPERITY : SMOOTH ::
   (a) color : blue
   (b) taste : sweet
   (c) chill : warm
   (d) anger : resentful

6. GRATUITOUS : NECESSARY ::
   (a) spurious : fake
   (b) ancient : old
   (c) doleful : happy
   (d) unusual : peculiar

7. EXTROVERT : SHY ::
   (a) buffoon : ridiculous
   (b) genius : unintelligent
   (c) athlete : fit
   (d) introvert : timid

8. SPURIOUS : GENUINE ::
   (a) unremitting : constant
   (b) garish : flamboyant
   (c) implacable : relentless
   (d) rambunctious : placid

adjudicate

centennial

countenance

disgruntle

equilibrium

expedite

gird

gratuitous

illusory

implacable

luminary

manifesto

mesmerize

precedent

spurious

9. HIERARCHY : LEADER ::

(a) pyramid : apex   (c) sphere : circle

(b) earth : equator   (d) nation : flag

10. BUFFOON : SERIOUSNESS ::

(a) sprinter : speed   (c) scientist: knowledge

(b) invalid : health   (d) plant : sunshine

2D Images of Words

Circle the letter of each sentence that suggests the numbered bold vocabulary word. In each group, you may circle more than one letter or none at all.

1. **centennial**

(a) In 1996, Utah celebrated its 1896 admission to the Union.

(b) The square root of 100 is 10.

(c) One hundred Mexican centavos make up one Mexican peso.

2. **manifesto**

(a) Holly was unable to come to school today because she's home with a cold.

(b) The striking miners published their demands in a statement that outlined their fourteen concerns.

(c) The title of the pamphlet was "The Reform Party's Ideology."

3. **expedite**

(a) To make sure it got there on time, I delivered the package myself.

(b) Light from the sun takes about eight minutes to reach the earth.

(c) Lewis and Clark's party set off in 1803 to explore the West.

4. **countenance**

(a) The final vote was 219 votes in support of the motion and 121 against it.

(b) The sad face of a child peering from a window haunted Marlowe's dreams.

(c) Congress allowed the president's veto of the bill to go unchallenged.

5. **spurious**

(a) Scholars doubt the claim that George Washington never told a lie.

(b) This letter signed by Abraham Lincoln is dated April 15, 1866, one year after he died.

(c) Kassia probably never intended to keep her promise to host the meeting.

6. **illusory**

(a) Although they were losing 54–11 at halftime, the team still thought it could win the game.

(b) Her name was on the tip of my tongue, but I could not think of it.

(c) Jimmy is foolish to think that he will win the lottery.

7. **disgruntled**

(a) Passengers bumped from the flight demanded to speak to the airline's manager.

(b) When Liza is under stress, her stomach invariably gets upset.

(c) Al just rolled over and went back to sleep when his alarm clock went off.

8. **precedent**

(a) John Quincy Adams was the father of historian Charles Francis Adams.

(b) Remember the spelling rule that *i* comes before *e* except after *c*.

(c) In 1849, Elizabeth Blackwell became the first woman in the United States to receive a medical degree.

9. **implacable**

(a) Ever since their argument, they refuse to see each other.

(b) The townspeople finally gave up their efforts to save the beach from development.

(c) The Allies continued to wage war until Germany surrendered.

10. **mesmerized**

(a) Oblivious to his surroundings, Hamlet stared at the ghost of his father.

(b) The children climbed into bed and at once fell into a deep sleep.

(c) We sat frozen in our chairs as the magician performed amazing tricks.

adjudicate
centennial
countenance
disgruntle
equilibrium
expedite
gird
gratuitous
illusory
implacable
luminary
manifesto
mesmerize
precedent
spurious

2E Passage

Read the passage below; then complete the exercise that follows it.

Gustave Eiffel's Tower

Guy de Maupassant, the famous French short story and novel writer, supposedly lunched every day at one of the restaurants in the Eiffel Tower. He maintained that he ate there because that was the only place in the French capital where he could eat without having to look at the famous Paris landmark. Although this story is most likely **spurious**, de Maupassant and many other **luminaries** of the art world were, in fact, **implacably** opposed to the tower from the start. When work on it began in 1887, a group of **disgruntled** artists, writers, musicians, and architects issued a **manifesto** calling the proposed tower "monstrous" and "useless." In a **gratuitous** slap at the United States, they declared that a structure that "even the United States would not **countenance** surely dishonors Paris."

The late nineteenth century was the age of monumental iron structures. The famed Brooklyn Bridge had been completed in 1883, and the French government wanted something equally impressive for the 1889 World's Fair in Paris, which celebrated the **centennial** of the French Revolution. Over one hundred proposals were submitted, and the **adjudicators** declared Gustave Eiffel's proposal the winner. His plan called for a thousand-foot iron tower that would be the tallest structure in the world; it retained this title until the 1,046-foot Chrysler Building in New York was built in 1930.

The World's Fair was to open in May 1889; Eiffel signed the contract on January 8, 1887. He had just over two years to complete the project, and he moved **expeditiously**—work on the tower's foundations was completed in five months! In order to achieve this feat, 40,000 cubic yards of earth had to be removed, with each of the tower's four feet set in a 20-foot-thick base of concrete, limestone, and granite. Once the foundation was completed, the iron girders and other components, which were made in workshops three miles from the site, began arriving daily. When these were riveted together, the four corner sections began rising, leaning inward at an angle of 54 degrees, until they reached a height of 180 feet. At this point, a 25-foot-wide iron "belt" was used to **gird** them into a single structure. A similar operation was carried out at 380 feet, and from this platform, the four corners converged to form a single spire.

There was no **precedent** for such a massive structure in Paris. Many Parisians were **mesmerized** by the sight of the great iron tower getting taller by the day. Others expressed misgivings, fearing that the tower would topple in a strong wind. But such fears proved **illusory**. Fierce weather had no impact on the structure, which could easily support elevators as well as the numerous people they would carry to the top. In installing elevators, Eiffel did not choose a single, vertical elevator, which would have been simple to install but which would have cluttered the graceful open arches at the base of the tower. Instead, Eiffel placed elevators at two of the four corners.

The Eiffel Tower was a well-managed and remarkable feat of engineering. It was completed within the time allotted and within its $1.6 million budget. It is a huge structure, yet its curving shape is light and airy, giving it a sense of lift. At the same time, the tower appears to be firmly rooted in the earth. These two opposing elements work together in complete **equilibrium** to make France's great national monument a triumph of design.

Answer each of the following questions in the form of a sentence. If a question does not contain a vocabulary word from this lesson's word list, use one in your answer. Use each word only once.

1. Why might the story about de Maupassant be considered **spurious**?

2. How did Maupassant and some other **luminaries** feel about the Eiffel Tower?

3. Who issued a **manifesto** that claimed that the Eiffel Tower is "useless"?

4. What was the **gratuitous** insult made to the United States in the manifesto?

5. What did the 1889 World's Fair in Paris celebrate?

6. Who declared Gustave Eiffel the winner of the contest to create a monument for the 1889 World's Fair?

7. Did Paris have any structures as large as the Eiffel Tower?

8. How did some Parisians react to the tower?

9. How were the fears of the tower's toppling shown to be **illusory**?

10. Why is the Eiffel Tower called a "triumph of design" in the passage?

11. Describe Gustave Eiffel's possible **countenance** after he heard that his proposal was declared the winner.

12. Why were some people **disgruntled** about the tower?

FUN & FASCINATING FACTS

Centennial and *centenary* both mean a hundredth anniversary or refer to its celebration. *Centennial* is the preferred American form, while *centenary* is more common in Britain. Both are formed from the Latin word *centum*, which means "one hundred." Both can take the prefixes *bi-*, "two," *tri-*, "three," or *quadri-*, "four," to indicate multiples of one hundred years. Since Mozart died on December 5, 1791, the *bicentenary* of his death occurred in 1991. The year 2007 marks the *quadricentennial* of the founding of Jamestown, Virginia, in 1607.

Countenance can be a noun, meaning "facial expression," or a verb, meaning "to approve." Although these two meanings seem quite different, they are, in fact, related. The initial meaning of *countenance* was "facial expression." Because we can show our approval with a favorable facial expression, the meaning "to approve" was later taken as an additional meaning of *countenance*.

Around two hundred years ago, an Austrian physician named Mesmer discovered hypnosis as a new way of treating patients. He called it "animal magnetism." But one of Mesmer's pupils coined the word **mesmerize** to describe this treatment. When *hypnotize* later came into use, *mesmerize* took on its present meaning.

Lesson 3

Word List   Study the definitions of the words below; then do the exercises for the lesson.

curtail
kər tāl´

v. To cut short or reduce.
The performance was **curtailed** when a fire broke out in the theater.

discriminate
di skrim´ i nāt

v. 1. To make or recognize clear distinctions.
During hunting season, it's prudent for hikers to wear orange so that hunters can easily **discriminate** between people and other animals.
2. To treat in a less or more favorable way.
Some employers still **discriminate** against women by paying them less than their male counterparts.
discrimination *n.* 1. The recognizing of clear distinctions.
It's helpful to make a **discrimination** between what you think you want and what you really need.
2. The act of making a distinction in favor of or against a person or thing on the basis of the group or category rather than according to actual merit.
Federal law prohibits **discrimination** based on race or creed.
3. The act of making fine distinctions; good or refined taste.
Your penchant for garish attire shows a lack of **discrimination**.

espionage
es´ pē ə näzh

n. 1. The act of spying, especially a government spy obtaining secrets of another government.
Counterintelligence specialists use their knowledge of high-tech spying equipment to thwart acts of **espionage**.

inalienable
in āl´ yən ə bəl

adj. Not able to be taken or given away.
United States citizens are promised certain **inalienable** rights that are spelled out in the Bill of Rights, the first ten amendments to the Constitution.

incarcerate
in kär´ sər āt

v. To confine or to put in prison.
Maximum security prisoners were **incarcerated** on Alcatraz, an island in San Francisco Bay, until 1963.
incarceration *n.*
His **incarceration** lasted five years, after which he was a free man.

indignity
in dig´ nə tē

n. An insult to one's pride; offensive or humiliating treatment.
His mother waited until they got home to reprimand her son, in order to spare him the **indignity** of being criticized in front of his friends.

indiscriminate
in di skrim´ i nət

adj. Not marked by careful distinctions; haphazard.
She was an **indiscriminate** reader and devoured everything from comics to history books.

infamous
in´ fə məs

adj. 1. Having a very bad reputation; notorious.
The CIA's **infamous** agent, Aldrich Ames, sold compromising information to the Soviets that cost the lives of many Soviet secret agents.
2. Disgraceful; vicious.
The defendant was charged with an **infamous** crime.
infamy *n.* (in´ fə mē)
The assassination of Abraham Lincoln was an act of **infamy**.

intercede
in tər sēd´

v. To act or plead on another's behalf; to try to smooth the differences between two parties.
Instead of **interceding**, my parents encouraged my brother and me to resolve our differences on our own.

malign
mə līn´

v. To say negative and unfair things about; slander.
The proprietor thought **maligning** his competitor's products would boost his own sales.
adj. Evil; showing ill will.
The **malign** look he gave me expressed his anger.

perpetrate
pur´ pə trāt

v. To commit, as a crime or other antisocial act.
The con artist was guilty of **perpetrating** a minor scam.
perpetrator *n.*
I couldn't figure out who the **perpetrator** was until the end of the mystery.

rampant
ram´ pənt

adj. Threateningly wild, without restraint or control; widespread.
The **rampant** vines covered the slope and began to climb the surrounding trees.

rancor
raŋ´ kər

n. A deep, long-held feeling of hatred or bitterness.
His **rancor** for the group turned him into its implacable foe.

reparation
rep ər ā´ shən

n. 1. A mending or repair.
The building needed major **reparation** after the tornado.
2. (usually plural) A making up or payment for a wrong or damage done, especially in the case of an international war.
Iraq was required to pay **reparations** to Kuwait after the Gulf War.

smattering
smat´ ər iŋ

n. 1. Superficial, scattered knowledge.
He picked up a **smattering** of Spanish while in Mexico.
2. A small amount.
She wrote thousands of letters, of which only a **smattering** have been published.

3A Understanding Meanings

Read the sentences below. If a sentence correctly uses the word in bold, write *C* on the line below it. If a sentence is incorrect, rewrite it so that the vocabulary word in bold is used correctly.

1. Something that is **inalienable** is so strange that it's unrecognizable.

_____

2. To **intercede** is to seize something while it is on its way.

_____

3. **Reparations** are compensation for injury caused.

_____

4. **Incarceration** is the act of burning something to ashes.

5. To **perpetrate** a rumor is to keep repeating it so that it doesn't die down.

6. To **discriminate** is to perceive differences.

7. An **indignity** is something that boosts one's self-esteem.

8. A **smattering** is an exchange of gossip or idle talk.

9. To **curtail** someone's authority is to diminish it.

10. **Infamous** behavior is shocking or brutal.

11. A **rampant** disease is one that spreads wildly.

12. To **malign** something is to make sure it is straight.

13. **Rancor** is deep, long-standing spite.

14. **Espionage** is the obtaining of information by spying.

curtail
discriminate
espionage
inalienable
incarcerate
indignity
indiscriminate
infamous
intercede
malign
perpetrate
rampant
rancor
reparation
smattering

15. An **indiscriminate** policy is one that ignores particular circumstances.

3B Using Words

If the word (or a form of the word) in bold fits in a sentence in the group below it, write the word in the blank. If the word does not fit, leave the space empty.

1. **discriminate**

   (a) It's difficult to _____ the different colors in this poor light.

   (b) We do not _____ against older persons in our hiring practices.

   (c) A five-year-old may be too young to _____ clearly between right and wrong.

2. **intercede**

   (a) When Carmen needed a new job, I offered to _____ on her behalf.

   (b) I was able to _____ the package before it was delivered.

   (c) If the rain stops, the floodwaters will begin to _____ in a day or so.

3. **malign**

   (a) I will not allow him to _____ my friend with these spurious stories.

   (b) Despite his denials, I believe he acted out of _____ motives.

   (c) Bryant must improve these _____ test scores if he wants to go to college.

4. **reparation**

   (a) The damage to the property was so great as to be beyond _____ .

   (b) Lawrence's neighbor was ordered to pay him $1,000 as _____ for the damage she caused to his lawn.

   (c) Joey received a small _____ for helping out around the farm.

5. **inalienable**

   (a) Freedom of speech is considered to be an _____ right in the United States.

   (b) Mark's _____ attitude makes him appear unusually competent.

   (c) It is an _____ rule in this house that family members take turns washing dishes.

6. **infamous**

   (a) It's hard to remain _____ when you're the winner of the Nobel Peace Prize.

   (b) Several books have been written about the _____ crime boss Al Capone.

   (c) Appearing on late-night talk shows is an _____ act.

7. **rampant**

    (a) Illegal drug use became _____ as social conditions deteriorated.

    (b) Traffic on the highway is especially _____ during the morning rush hours.

    (c) The bull, _____ and ready to charge at any moment, snorted fiercely.

8. **indiscriminate**

    (a) Some cats are quite _____ about what they bring into the house.

    (b) The _____ use of pesticides caused great harm to wildlife.

    (c) Charlie's parents are concerned about his _____ television viewing habits.

3C Word Study

Choose from the two words provided and use each word only once. One space should be left blank.

curtail/reduce

1. Candidates will _____ political activity during the period of official mourning.

2. If you _____ the price to a dollar apiece, you'll sell more.

3. Global warming causes the polar ice caps to _____ .

equilibrium/balance

4. The Treaty of Vienna maintained Europe's political _____ for a century.

5. The ball begins to drop when it loses its _____ .

6. Sue lost her _____ while learning to walk on stilts.

rampant/widespread

7. By 1800, the use of paper money was _____ throughout North America.

8. Under these appallingly dirty conditions, it's no wonder that disease was _____ .

9. The rooms in the palace were _____ with gold plating.

gratuitous/unnecessary

10. Leaving a tip for excellent service is _____ .

11. Calling your uncle "Old Scrooge" was an unkind and _____ remark.

12. The mechanic denied performing _____ car repairs.

spurious/false

13. The police questioned the man in the blue van, but it turned out to be a _____ lead.

14. Half of her answers were correct and half were _____ .

15. These counterfeit hundred-dollar bills are _____ currency.

curtail
discriminate
espionage
inalienable
incarcerate
indignity
indiscriminate
infamous
intercede
malign
perpetrate
rampant
rancor
reparation
smattering

3D Images of Words

Circle the letter of each sentence that suggests the numbered bold vocabulary word. In each group, you may circle more than one letter or none at all.

1. **curtail**

   (a) The store closes three hours earlier during the off-season.

   (b) My grandparents often go on long road trips in the spring.

   (c) Major suppliers have cut the cost of heating oil by five cents a gallon.

2. **perpetrate**

   (a) We found out it was the boy next door who made those crank phone calls.

   (b) Scholars argue about who really started World War I.

   (c) They take pride in maintaining their family traditions.

3. **rancor**

   (a) I'll never forgive Sandy for betraying my trust.

   (b) The apple was so sour that I was unable to take more than one bite.

   (c) The discussion was marred by wild accusations of criminal wrongdoing.

4. **indignity**

   (a) Ruby objected strongly when a boy tried to get in front of her in line.

   (b) Sam felt foolish riding a donkey when everyone else was riding beautiful horses.

   (c) It was unfair of the club owner to fire the manager in public.

5. **espionage**

   (a) The foreign agent was caught in the act taking photographs of top-secret documents.

   (b) Secret wiretaps revealed the nation's confidential plans.

   (c) The covert destruction of property was an act of cowardice.

6. **discrimination**

   (a) Cara is careful to choose books that are at the right reading level for her students.

   (b) The thief gave the police the names of those who had helped him break in.

   (c) There were once separate drinking fountains for "whites" and "coloreds" in the United States.

7. **intercede**

   (a) Cinderella got help from her fairy godmother when she needed it most.

   (b) The medicine the doctor gave me had me on my feet in no time.

   (c) My application would have been rejected had it not been for Beth's recommendation letter.

8. **smattering**

   (a) She knew just enough Portuguese to get by while she was in Lisbon.

   (b) Of the ninety plays he wrote, fewer than six have survived.

   (c) Marla didn't see the banana on the street and rolled right over it with her bike.

9. **indiscriminate**

   (a) Men and women should be treated equally when it comes to promotions and pay.

   (b) The jury found the defendant not guilty, and he was promptly released.

   (c) Joe is not a fussy eater; he enjoys whatever he is given.

10. **incarceration**

   (a) The fire totally destroyed the building as well as its valuable contents.

   (b) The penalty was five years in prison without parole.

   (c) The prisoners were held in the old mill until they could be transferred.

3E Passage

Read the passage below; then complete the exercise that follows it.

Yoshiko Uchida: Second-Class Citizen?

curtail
discriminate
espionage
inalienable
incarcerate
indignity
indiscriminate
infamous
intercede
malign
perpetrate
rampant
rancor
reparation
smattering

Although their parents had been born in Japan, Yoshiko Uchida and her older sister, Keiko, were American citizens from birth. The girls spoke only a **smattering** of Japanese and grew up in Berkeley, California, in the 1930s as typical American teenagers, believing that they possessed the **inalienable** right to life, liberty, and the pursuit of happiness promised to all Americans. But when Japan launched its **infamous** attack on the United States fleet at Pearl Harbor, Hawaii, on December 7, 1941, they discovered that they were mistaken.

Of course, the Uchida sisters deserved no blame for the actions of Japan's military leaders, but they suffered from the anti-Japanese feeling that was suddenly **rampant** among the populace. Japanese Americans were **maligned** as potential traitors and suspected of conspiring to commit acts of **espionage** for a country with which the United States was now at war.

Within hours of the attack, United States government agents searched the Uchida home and took Yoshiko's father away without disclosing what he was accused of or where he was being taken. He was one of many Japanese Americans placed in similar circumstances who had broken no law and were never charged with any offense. This was merely the first of the many **indignities** suffered by Yoshiko's family. The right to travel freely was severely **curtailed** for all Japanese Americans on the West Coast. They were forced to observe an eight o'clock curfew and were forbidden to go more than five miles from their homes. They were also ordered to turn in all cameras, binoculars, short-wave radios, and firearms.

On May 1, 1942, by order of President Roosevelt, 120,000 people of Japanese descent living on the West Coast, two-thirds of them American citizens, were **indiscriminately** rounded up and were allowed to take only what they could carry. The Uchida family was among those forced to leave. Yoshiko's studies—she had been close to getting a degree in education at the University of California, Berkeley—were abruptly terminated. She had no idea when, if ever, she would be allowed to resume her education.

The Uchidas were taken to a nearby makeshift prison camp, where Mr. Uchida was permitted to rejoin his family. After being held there for four months, the family was moved to a prison camp near Delta, Utah, on the edge of the Sevier Desert. The camp, called Topaz, was surrounded by barbed wire, with watchtowers at each corner. It was one of ten such camps throughout the United States, hastily set up to detain Japanese Americans.

Thanks to friends on the outside who **interceded** on their behalf, and because the hysteria against Japanese Americans had abated somewhat, the **incarceration** of Yoshiko and Keiko Uchida at Topaz lasted less than a year. Yoshiko was given leave to attend school at Smith College in Massachusetts, and Keiko was given a position at the Department of Education's nursery school at nearby Mount Holyoke College. Later, as investigation into their backgrounds showed them to be blameless, their parents were allowed to leave Topaz and were soon reunited with their daughters.

Yoshiko's father never permitted himself to feel **rancor** against his adopted country for the wrong it had **perpetrated** against Japanese Americans. He believed that one day the government would admit it had made a terrible mistake. That day finally came in 1988, when Congress voted to pay **reparations** to the surviving members of the uprooted families.

For Yoshiko, the experience of being treated like a second-class citizen was not easily forgotten, but she used the experience positively. Yoshiko became a prolific writer; many of the books and short stories she wrote help to educate others about the unjust treatment of Japanese Americans during World War II. These stories not only convey the alienation and rejection felt by all victims of **discrimination**; they also serve as necessary reminders of the terrible consequences that result from denying someone or a whole group of people the fundamental rights meant to be enjoyed by all Americans.

Answer each of the following questions in the form of a sentence. If a question does not contain a vocabulary word from this lesson's word list, use one in your answer. Use each word only once.

1. Why would the Uchida sisters have had difficulty communicating in Japanese?

2. When did Japan begin its **infamous** attack on Pearl Harbor?

3. What public sentiments followed this attack?

4. What were some of the freedoms that were **curtailed** for Japanese Americans?

5. Why were radios, cameras, and guns taken from people of Japanese descent?

6. What information in the passage suggests that the United States government did not **discriminate** between Japanese Americans who were loyal to the United States and those who might have been loyal to Japan?

7. What was the first of the **indignities** suffered by the Uchida family during this time?

8. What brought Yoshiko's and Keiko's period of imprisonment to an end?

9. What information in the passage suggests that Mr. Uchida was not embittered by the unjust treatment he endured during the war with Japan?

10. How did the United States government acknowledge that its treatment of Japanese Americans during the war was a mistake?

FUN & FASCINATING FACTS

To **curtail** something is to cut it short. A *tailor* is a person who cuts cloth and sews it into garments. What do the words *curtail* and *tailor* have in common? Both were derived from the Middle English word *taillen*, meaning "to cut." Middle English was the language spoken in England between about 1100 and 1500.

The Latin word *malus* means "bad" or "evil" and is related to the root of many English words. *Malice* is a feeling of ill will toward another; a *malady* is a sickness or disease; a *malefactor* is a criminal or wrongdoer; a *malignant* tumor is one that could cause death; a doctor guilty of *malpractice* has done harm to a patient. And, of course, to **malign** someone is to say bad things about that person.

Lesson 4

Word List
Study the definitions of the words below; then do the exercises for the lesson.

accolade
ak´ ə lād

n. An expression of approval or respect for special merit; an award.
In England, knighthood is a high **accolade** given for service to the state.

adamant
ad´ ə mənt

adj. Not yielding; firm.
I missed the TV show because of my mother's **adamant** refusal to let me watch television before I'm done with my homework.

adulate
a´ joō lāt

v. To flatter or admire excessively; to idolize.
Opera lovers **adulate** the Mexican singing sensation Rosaria Rosario; her performances are often sold out.
adulation *n.*
Members of the crowd showed their **adulation** by giving the performers a standing ovation.

altercation
ôl tər kā´ shən

n. A loud and determined dispute; a noisy quarrel.
After the hockey player purposely tripped a member of the opposing team, an **altercation** broke out.

annals
an´ əlz

n. pl. A historical record of events, often arranged in a yearly sequence.
I can easily research the history of my town because its **annals** have been preserved consistently since 1685.

assiduous
ə sij´ oō əs

adj. Diligent and persistent.
Maureen was the most **assiduous** researcher in our biology lab.

chary
chăr´ ē

adj. Exercising caution; hesitant.
Be **chary** about making promises that you might not be able to keep.

clique
klik

n. A small, exclusive group; a group held together by like interests or purpose.
The new student found it difficult to fit in at the high school because many of the students there belonged to **cliques** that didn't welcome newcomers.

decrepit
dē krep´ it

adj. Worn-out with use; broken-down.
The **decrepit** buildings were torn down and replaced with a modern apartment complex.

endow
en dou´

v. To provide with a quality, a thing, or a gift of money.
Connie was **endowed** with a beautiful singing voice.
endowment *n.*
The college receives much of its support from **endowments** established by alumni.

ephemeral
e fem´ ər əl

adj. Lasting a very short time.
The pleasures of our few days in the mountains were **ephemeral**, with only a faint memory remaining.

ingratiate
in grā´ shē āt

v. To work to gain the favor of someone.
He attempted to **ingratiate** himself with his teacher by helping out after class.

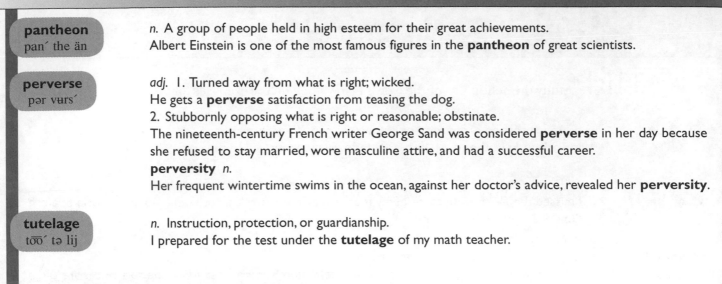

pantheon
pan´ the än

n. A group of people held in high esteem for their great achievements.
Albert Einstein is one of the most famous figures in the **pantheon** of great scientists.

perverse
pər vurs´

adj. 1. Turned away from what is right; wicked.
He gets a **perverse** satisfaction from teasing the dog.
2. Stubbornly opposing what is right or reasonable; obstinate.
The nineteenth-century French writer George Sand was considered **perverse** in her day because she refused to stay married, wore masculine attire, and had a successful career.
perversity *n.*
Her frequent wintertime swims in the ocean, against her doctor's advice, revealed her **perversity**.

tutelage
tōō´ tə lij

n. Instruction, protection, or guardianship.
I prepared for the test under the **tutelage** of my math teacher.

4A Understanding Meanings

Read the sentences below. If a sentence correctly uses the word in bold, write *C* on the line of the line below. If a sentence is incorrect, rewrite it so that the vocabulary word in bold is used correctly.

1. To **endow** a library is to provide money for its upkeep.

2. A **decrepit** vehicle is one in a state of disrepair.

3. A **pantheon** is a kind of motor vehicle.

accolade
adamant
adulate
altercation
annals
assiduous
chary
clique
decrepit
endow
ephemeral
ingratiate
pantheon
perverse
tutelage

4. An **altercation** is an angry argument.

5. **Ephemeral** pleasures are those that are short-lived.

6. **Tutelage** is a fee charged for providing a service.

7. To **adulate** someone is to try to copy what that person does.

8. A **clique** is a quick, sharp sound.

9. A person **chary** of praise is slow to accept it.

10. An **accolade** is a recognition of merit.

11. An **assiduous** person is one who perseveres.

12. A **perverse** response is one that seems improper or unreasonable.

13. To **ingratiate** oneself is to work to gain favor.

14. Most **annals** are yearly publications.

15. To be **adamant** is to be open to compromise.

4B Using Words

If the word (or a form of the word) in bold fits in a sentence in the group below it, write the word in the blank. If the word does not fit, leave the space empty.

1. **assiduous**

   (a) The _____ look she gave me suggested she was hiding something.

   (b) The hotel staff are _____ in attending to the comfort of guests.

   (c) An _____ search failed to turn up my missing homework.

2. endow

(a) A good writer can take a word and _____ it with new meaning.

(b) Sonia used her vast fortune to _____ a number of local colleges.

(c) Taylor frequently _____ back and forth because she was so indecisive.

3. adamant

(a) The doctor was _____ that there was nothing wrong with Fred's health.

(b) Ryan's _____ refusal convinced us that he was unlikely to change his mind.

(c) It was _____ to me that we were wasting our time trying to start the car.

4. perverse

(a) Increasingly _____ weather caused us to postpone our sailing trip.

(b) Jiang is so _____ he cannot agree to anything we suggest.

(c) It is _____ to let criminals profit from books in which they write about their crimes.

5. clique

(a) I could hear the _____ of the pool balls coming from the next room.

(b) The government was led by a small _____ of presidential advisers.

(c) The _____ grew rapidly and soon numbered in the hundreds of thousands.

6. adulation

(a) Shouts of _____ came from the crowd when the band appeared on stage.

(b) Poets of the 1800s received the same _____ that movie stars get today.

(c) Charles Dickens basked in the _____ of his American audiences.

7. altercation

(a) Road construction caused a traffic _____ that stretched for over two miles.

(b) The _____ arose over a dispute as to who was responsible for the damage.

(c) A feeling of _____ swept over Miska when she realized she was alone.

8. chary

(a) _____ investors are not rushing to buy this latest stock.

(b) Whitney is _____ about eating at that restaurant because a group of its customers once complained of food poisoning.

(c) Let us be _____ of criticizing the proposal until we have examined it.

accolade
adamant
adulate
altercation
annals
assiduous
chary
clique
decrepit
endow
ephemeral
ingratiate
pantheon
perverse
tutelage

4C Word Study

The prefixes *in-* and *im-* can mean "not," changing a word to its opposite. However, the letters *in* and *im* do not always indicate a prefix. In the spaces provided, write a brief definition of each of the words below. Write "yes" if the letters *in* and *im* indicate the prefix meaning "not" in each word.

1. imbue   _____   _____

2. implacable   _____   _____

3. incarcerate   _____   _____

4. indiscriminate _____   _____

5. ingratiate   _____   _____

6. intercede   _____   _____

7. instigate   _____   _____

8. inalienable   _____   _____

9. indignity   _____   _____

10. infamous   _____   _____

4D Images of Words

Circle the letter of each sentence that suggests the numbered bold vocabulary word. In each group, you may circle more than one letter or none at all.

1. **clique**

   (a) Jeremy and Lauren liked each other from the start and have remained fast friends.

   (b) To join the club you must be sponsored by two active members.

   (c) The cave was dark and damp.

2. **annals**

   (a) The rock band's concert was sold out last night.

   (b) I looked in the library to find that novel you told me about.

   (c) The records of baseball's National League go back to 1876.

3. **accolade**

   (a) He slapped me on the back and said, "Well done, Carlos. I'm proud of you."

   (b) The Pulitzer Prize is journalism's highest honor.

   (c) Cobb's play received a rave review from the *New York Times's* drama critic.

4. **tutelage**

(a) I received flying lessons from a former navy test pilot.

(b) He gave credit for his fine education to his devoted English teacher.

(c) Meg yelled after me as I left, "Don't forget the rehearsal tonight!"

5. **pantheon**

(a) Jane Austen is arguably one of the most esteemed novelists in English literature.

(b) Alain was pleased when he was named Employee of the Month.

(c) Joe Louis and Muhammad Ali are two of the greatest names in boxing.

6. **decrepit**

(a) The bus was so old we were sure it would break down before going far.

(b) He took one look at the sofa and said I'd be lucky to get ten dollars for it.

(c) We were unsure whether to have our old refrigerator fixed and pay a huge repair bill, or to get a new one.

7. **adamant**

(a) Breaking up boulders with sledgehammers was hard, unpleasant work.

(b) The algebra course was so hard that at times I felt like dropping it.

(c) She looked me squarely in the eye and said, "Absolutely not!"

8. **perverse**

(a) Whenever we said we liked something, Suzie spoke out against it.

(b) It seemed odd that a former Ku Klux Klansman was made a federal judge.

(c) "You don't like flowers!" I exclaimed. "How can you not like flowers?"

9. **ephemeral**

(a) She had her own TV show in the 1980s but then dropped from public view.

(b) We had a fifteen-minute wait before the train arrived.

(c) The vinegar fly completes its entire life cycle in ten days.

10. **ingratiate**

(a) I can't believe that Deena never even thanked you for your assistance.

(b) Jonas praised his boss at every opportunity.

(c) "My, what a thoughtful daughter you have," the professor said to the university president.

accolade
adamant
adulate
altercation
annals
assiduous
chary
clique
decrepit
endow
ephemeral
ingratiate
pantheon
perverse
tutelage

4E Passage

Read the passage below; then complete the exercise that follows it.

A Most Valuable Person

Success in the sports world can be painfully **ephemeral**. Athletes understand only too well that the crowd's **adulation** one day can turn all too quickly to rancorous jeers the next. But once or twice in a generation, a player emerges whose fame seems destined to last for as long as the game is played. In the **annals** of baseball, Roberto Clemente is one such athlete.

Born in Puerto Rico in 1934, Clemente dreamed of playing professional baseball. As a child, it was evident that he was **endowed** with great natural ability, yet no one practiced the necessary skills with bat and ball more **assiduously** than he. Clemente hit the ball accurately and with ever increasing power as he matured, and he moved with incredible speed between the bases and in the outfield. At eighteen, he signed his first professional contract with the Puerto Rican league; at twenty, he signed with the Pittsburgh Pirates and played as a right fielder with them for eighteen outstanding seasons.

Clemente was often lonely in his early years as a professional. He spoke little English when he first came to the United States and found that this language barrier excluded him from the tightly knit groups that ballplayers form. He was further ostracized by the press, which would sometimes refer to him as the "dusky flyer" or the "chocolate-covered islander." A number of reporters seemed to find his less-than-perfect English comical and took a **perverse** pleasure in misquoting him. Not surprisingly, Clemente, who was proud of his heritage, frequently had **altercations** with the press and was **chary** of giving interviews. Unfortunately, this only earned him a reputation for aloofness.

He never tried to **ingratiate** himself with the press. He had no need to, because as one outstanding season followed another, his record spoke for itself. In 1966, he became the first Latino ballplayer to be voted the Most Valuable Player. In the 1971 World Series against the Baltimore Orioles, he batted .414 and was named the series's Most Valuable Player. The next year he joined baseball's **pantheon** when his lifetime total of base hits reached 3,000, a feat achieved by only ten other players.

Clemente was committed to making a contribution to the island of his birth. Instead of taking off the winter months to relax, he returned to Puerto Rico, year after year, to play in the winter league, thereby giving aspiring youngsters a chance to see their idol up close. He took a personal interest in talented young players, and under his **tutelage**, many went on to successful careers in the major leagues. Clemente also dreamed of creating a sports complex in Puerto Rico; he decided that he would devote his energies to this project after his retirement. But that opportunity never came.

In December, 1972, an earthquake shattered the Nicaraguan capital of Managua. Clemente at once organized a relief effort for the survivors. A **decrepit** DC-7 cargo plane, donated for the operation, was filled with food and medical supplies. Friends, worried about his safety, urged him not to make the trip, but he was **adamant** that his presence was necessary to ensure that the supplies were not diverted to the hands of the country's corrupt ruling **clique**. Shortly after takeoff, the plane lost power and crashed into the sea. No one survived.

The following year, Clemente's number, 21, was retired by the Pirates, and Clemente received baseball's highest **accolade**—acceptance into the Baseball Hall of Fame. He was the first Latino player to be so honored. His dream of a sports complex was taken up by his wife, Vera. She worked tirelessly to make it a reality, and today, the Roberto Clemente Sports City occupies 304 acres in Carolina, the town where Clemente was born. Vera Clemente is its director, and more than 100,000 children enjoy its extensive facilities.

Answer each of the following questions in the form of a sentence. If a question does not contain a vocabulary word from this lesson's word list, use one in your answer. Use each word only once.

1. Explain how success in sports can be **ephemeral**.

2. How was Clemente's childhood a promising start for him as an athlete?

3. What evidence in the passage suggests that Clemente resented the press?

4. What did the reporters do that contributed to Clemente's unease with them?

5. Why was it especially unnecessary for Clemente to **ingratiate** himself with the press?

6. What happened when Clemente reached a total of 3,000 base hits?

7. How did Clemente try to help talented youngsters with an interest in baseball?

8. Why did Clemente's friends attempt to persuade him not to go to Nicaragua?

9. How did Clemente respond to his friends' warnings?

10. What happened in the year following Clemente's death?

FUN & FASCINATING FACTS

The ancient Greeks used the word **adamant** to describe an imaginary stone so hard that nothing could penetrate or shatter it. The word has survived in modern English as a synonym for *stubborn* or *unyielding*. *Adamantine* is used to describe literal hardness, as that of a diamond or certain metals.

An **altercation** is a quarrel or noisy argument, but note that it is purely verbal. An *altercation* may escalate into violence, and when it ceases to be verbal and becomes physical, it is then a fight or a brawl.

Annals is a plural noun for which there is no singular form. The word is derived from the Latin *annalis*, which means "yearly"—an indication that *annals* are records of events kept from year to year.

The **Pantheon** (with a capital *p*) is a circular temple, built in Rome in 27 B.C., to honor all the Roman gods. The name is formed from two Greek words, *pan-*, "all," and *theos*, meaning "god." The term is used literally to describe a public building to honor the illustrious citizens of a country, as is the Pantheon in Paris, completed in 1781. It is also used metaphorically to include collectively the names of individuals who have made significant contributions in a particular field of endeavor, such as science, politics, or sports. For this meaning, it is written *pantheon*, with a small *p*.

Review for Lessons 1-4

Crossword Puzzle Solve the crossword puzzle below by studying the clues and filling in the answer boxes. Clues followed by a number are definitions of words in Lessons 1 through 4. The number gives the word list in which the answer to the clue appears.

Clues Across

1. Sharpness or harshness of manner (1)

3. To encircle, bind, or surround (2)

5. To fill completely with a feeling or idea (1)

8. To cut short or reduce (3)

9. Widespread (3)

11. A historical record of events (4)

12. A small, exclusive group (4)

14. Opposite of *there*

16. Full of sorrow (1)

17. To weaken or ruin by degrees (1)

19. English river that runs through London

21. A person's face (2)

22. To facilitate (2)

24. A clown (1)

25. Not yielding; firm (4)

26. *A, E, I, O,* or *U*

Clues Down

1. An expression of approval or respect for special merit (4)

2. A person whose attention is focused on others (1)

3. Excessively bright and flashy (1)

4. Abbreviation for "dormitory"

6. Useful for finding one's way

7. Having a very bad reputation (3)

10. To say negative and unfair things about (3)

11. Excessive admiration (4)

13. Lasting a very short time (4)

15. Shade tree

18. A deep, long-held feeling of hate or bitterness (3)

20. To provide with a gift of money (4)

21. A detective looks for a _____

23. Same as 15 down

Lesson 5

> ## Word List
Study the definitions of the words below; then do the exercises for the lesson.

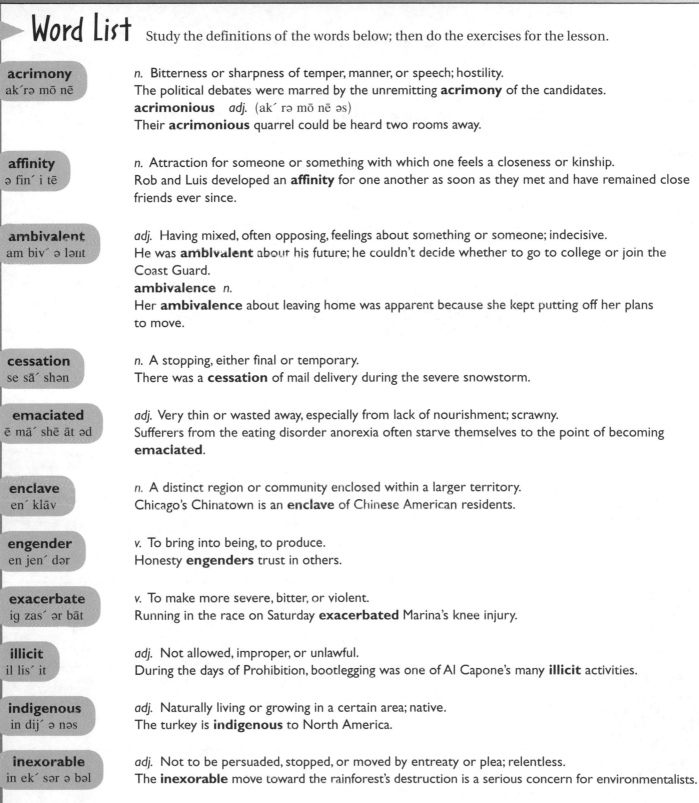

acrimony
ak´rə mō nē

n. Bitterness or sharpness of temper, manner, or speech; hostility.
The political debates were marred by the unremitting **acrimony** of the candidates.
acrimonious *adj.* (ak´ rə mō nē əs)
Their **acrimonious** quarrel could be heard two rooms away.

affinity
ə fin´ i tē

n. Attraction for someone or something with which one feels a closeness or kinship.
Rob and Luis developed an **affinity** for one another as soon as they met and have remained close friends ever since.

ambivalent
am biv´ ə lənt

adj. Having mixed, often opposing, feelings about something or someone; indecisive.
He was **ambivalent** about his future; he couldn't decide whether to go to college or join the Coast Guard.
ambivalence *n.*
Her **ambivalence** about leaving home was apparent because she kept putting off her plans to move.

cessation
se sā´ shən

n. A stopping, either final or temporary.
There was a **cessation** of mail delivery during the severe snowstorm.

emaciated
ē mā´ shē āt əd

adj. Very thin or wasted away, especially from lack of nourishment; scrawny.
Sufferers from the eating disorder anorexia often starve themselves to the point of becoming **emaciated**.

enclave
en´ klāv

n. A distinct region or community enclosed within a larger territory.
Chicago's Chinatown is an **enclave** of Chinese American residents.

engender
en jen´ dər

v. To bring into being, to produce.
Honesty **engenders** trust in others.

exacerbate
ig zas´ ər bāt

v. To make more severe, bitter, or violent.
Running in the race on Saturday **exacerbated** Marina's knee injury.

illicit
il lis´ it

adj. Not allowed, improper, or unlawful.
During the days of Prohibition, bootlegging was one of Al Capone's many **illicit** activities.

indigenous
in dij´ ə nəs

adj. Naturally living or growing in a certain area; native.
The turkey is **indigenous** to North America.

inexorable
in ek´ sər ə bəl

adj. Not to be persuaded, stopped, or moved by entreaty or plea; relentless.
The **inexorable** move toward the rainforest's destruction is a serious concern for environmentalists.

infatuated
in fach´ ōō āt əd

adj. Filled with excessive, shallow, or foolish love or desire.
My parents are **infatuated** with the idea of sailing around the world, so they attend every boat show they can.
infatuation *n.*
His **infatuation** with her lasted only a couple of weeks before he developed a crush on another girl.

insatiable
in sā´ shə bəl

adj. Never satisfied; greedy.
My nephew is endowed with an **insatiable** curiosity and is constantly asking questions.

poignant
poin´ yənt

adj. Painfully moving, affecting, or touching.
The **poignant** ending of the movie brought tears to my eyes.

proselytize
präs´ ə li tīz

v. To convert someone to a faith, belief, or cause.
She's an adamant socialist; she's always trying to **proselytize** people she meets.

5A Understanding Meanings

Read the sentences below. If a sentence correctly uses the word in bold, write *C* on the line below it. If a sentence is incorrect, rewrite it so that the vocabulary word in bold is used correctly.

1. To **engender** a change is to cause its occurrence.

2. An **illicit** practice is one that is illegal.

3. An **affinity** for something is an attraction to it.

acrimony
affinity
ambivalent
cessation
emaciated
enclave
engender
exacerbate
illicit
indigenous
inexorable
infatuated
insatiable
poignant
proselytize

4. **Infatuation** is an excessive fondness for something.

5. An **emaciated** person is one who has been set free.

6. A **poignant** story is one that is deeply moving.

7. An **enclave** is a small amount of resistance.

8. To **proselytize** is to talk someone into sharing one's beliefs.

9. The **cessation** of something is its stopping or coming to an end.

10. An **insatiable** longing is one that is soon satisfied.

11. **Ambivalence** is a change of heart.

12. To **exacerbate** a situation is to take steps to correct it.

13. An **inexorable** decision is one that is subject to change.

14. **Acrimony** is ill feeling indicated by hostility and harsh words.

15. An **indigenous** plant is one that is native to an area.

5B Using Words

If the word (or a form of the word) in bold fits in a sentence in the group below it, write the word in the blank. If the word does not fit, leave the space empty.

1. **enclave**

(a) Several heads of state attended the _____ that was held in Geneva.

(b) The rebels were confined to one small _____ in the mountains.

(c) Each ethnic group in the city inhabits its own little _____ .

2. **illicit**

   (a) Numerous letters and phone calls failed to _____ a reply.

   (b) The authorities attempted to stamp out the _____ hunting of elephants for their ivory tusks.

   (c) The funds were raised by _____ means and, therefore, must be returned to the donors.

3. **insatiable**

   (a) The _____ demand for grazing areas is destroying the world's forests.

   (b) The group claims to have almost _____ resources to put into the project.

   (c) He's very thin even though he has an _____ appetite.

4. **emaciated**

   (a) The soil in these parts is so _____ that nothing will grow.

   (b) Prolonged fasting had left him weak and _____ .

   (c) The soup they served was so _____ it tasted like cabbage water.

5. **affinity**

   (a) Her _____ for animals led her to consider becoming a veterinarian.

   (b) Parallel lines stretch to _____ without ever meeting.

   (c) Lincoln's _____ for politics showed itself at an early age.

6. **proselytize**

   (a) He _____ that the Bears would go to the Super Bowl within the next five years.

   (b) Group members _____ by going from door to door handing out pamphlets.

   (c) That society for animals encourages people to _____ on behalf of endangered species.

7. **inexorable**

   (a) He behaved _____ and disgusted everyone at the dinner table.

   (b) The _____ logic of your argument has convinced me.

   (c) We are concerned about the _____ growth of the world's population.

8. **engender**

   (a) Revolutions have a tendency to _____ a breakdown of all authority.

   (b) His manner and way of dressing _____ masculinity.

   (c) Lying _____ distrust.

acrimony
affinity
ambivalent
cessation
emaciated
enclave
engender
exacerbate
illicit
indigenous
inexorable
infatuated
insatiable
poignant
proselytize

5C Word Study

Fill in the missing word in each of the sentences below. Then write a brief definition of the word. The number in parentheses shows the lesson in which the word appears.

1. The prefix *ambi-* means "both." It combines with the Latin *valerere* (strong) to form the English word _____ (5).

   Definition: _____

2. The prefix *inter-* means "between." It combines with the Latin *cedere* (to go) to form the English word _____ (3).

   Definition: _____

3. The prefix *extro-* means "out" or "beyond" It combines with the Latin *vertere* (to turn) to form the English word _____ (1).

   Definition: _____

4. The prefix *equi-* means "equal." It combines with the Latin *libra* (balance) to form the English word _____ (2).

   Definition: _____

5. The prefix *epi-* means "close to." It combines with the Greek *hemera* (a day) to form the English word _____ (4).

   Definition: _____

6. The prefix *in-* sometimes means "not." It combines with the Latin *satiare* (to fill or satisfy) to form the English word _____ (5).

   Definition: _____

7. The prefix *in-* sometimes means "within." It combines with the Latin *fatuus* (foolish) to form the English word _____ (5).

   Definition: _____

8. The Latin *asper* means "rough." It forms the English word _____ (1).

   Definition: _____

9. The Latin *centum* means "one hundred." It combines with the Latin *annus* (year) to form the English word _____ (2).

   Definition: _____

10. The prefix *pre-* means "before." It combines with the Latin *cedere* (to go) to form the English

word _____ (2).

Definition: _____

5D Images of Words

Circle the letter of each sentence that suggests the numbered bold vocabulary word. In each group, you may circle more than one letter or none at all.

1. **ambivalence**

    (a) They want children, but the responsibility of being parents scares them.

    (b) The long pole she carries helps the tightrope walker to keep her balance.

    (c) The president was undecided whether to sign the bill or veto it.

2. **exacerbate**

    (a) Nan's decision not to apologize to her mother made a bad situation even worse.

    (b) The storm grew worse in the evening, making it impossible for us to leave.

    (c) Far from helping the patient, putting oil on the burn had just the opposite effect.

3. **poignant**

    (a) The pain in his abdomen was so severe that we rushed him to the hospital.

    (b) The scene in Romeo and Juliet where the lovers separate brought tears to the audience's eyes.

    (c) The painting captures the trusting look of a child gazing up at her mother.

4. **infatuation**

    (a) If pecan pie is on the menu, I find it impossible to resist ordering it.

    (b) In May, Sebastian was madly in love with Tara, but now he wants to marry Ana.

    (c) Bob's intense enthusiasm for painting soon ended, and now he's writing a novel.

5. **indigenous**

    (a) The United States is bordered by Canada to the north and Mexico to the south.

    (b) Cocoa trees—originally from Central America—have spread to other parts of the world.

    (c) Llamas are mammals from South America that are related to the Asian camel.

6. **cessation**

    (a) On December 20, 1860, South Carolina formally withdrew from the Union.

    (b) On April 9, 1865, war between the North and the South ended.

    (c) Midnight of December 31, 2000, marked the end of the twentieth century.

acrimony
affinity
ambivalent
cessation
emaciated
enclave
engender
exacerbate
illicit
indigenous
inexorable
infatuated
insatiable
poignant
proselytize

7. **acrimony**

   (a) They said angry things to each other that would have been better left unsaid.

   (b) Ms. Groves continues to receive a monthly check from her ex-husband.

   (c) Liza was so upset with Shawna that she said she never wanted to see her again.

8. **enclave**

   (a) They visited Little Italy, a largely Italian section of New York City.

   (b) They were pleasantly surprised to discover a small part of town where a group of artists lived and worked.

   (c) They ducked their heads to avoid the stalactites that were hanging from the ceiling of the cavern.

9. **affinity**

   (a) He grew up on a farm and has always been fond of animals.

   (b) Because of my fondness for chocolate, I gained a few pounds last year.

   (c) I felt close to my cousin at once even though it was our first meeting.

10. **illicit**

   (a) Despite the United States' total ban on trading with Iraq, some goods did get through.

   (b) American tourists who visited Cuba did so in defiance of United States law.

   (c) The reporter really pressed the celebrity for a chance to interview her.

5E Passage

Read the passage below; then complete the exercise that follows it.

A Vanishing Species

In a gesture intended to improve its strained and often **acrimonious** relationship with the United States, the Chinese government presented a pair of giant pandas to President Nixon in 1972. Not only did the gift **engender** warmer diplomatic relations between the two countries, but Ling-Ling and Hsing-Hsing became instant celebrities, triggering America's **infatuation** with giant pandas.

Resembling enormous, cuddly, black-and-white teddy bears with round, flat faces and large eye patches, giant pandas have become quite popular. Every city with a large zoo wants them because of the crowds they draw. In 1988, for example, the Toledo zoo paid China several hundred thousand dollars to rent a pair of pandas for five months. The public's desire for zoo tickets and panda-related products seemed **insatiable**. The zoo took in over three million dollars, and the city estimated that tourists drawn to the attraction brought in over sixty million dollars.

Zoos rent giant pandas, most often from China, but also from other American zoos, because the panda population is so limited and because their sale is severely restricted by law. According to 2004 estimates of the World Wildlife Fund (WWF), an organization that protects endangered species, about sixteen-hundred pandas are left in the wild. There are several hundred pandas in captivity, mainly in China's research or reserve centers. Giant pandas are **indigenous** to southeastern China, where a thousand years ago they roamed freely over two million square miles. Now restricted to twenty tiny **enclaves** in China, wild pandas inhabit less than a quarter of one percent of that area. Only three of these regions have populations exceeding one hundred, and some have fewer than twenty. The panda population was shrinking partially because its food supply has decreased. Pandas rely on the leaves and stalks of the arrow bamboo, which form the bulk of their diet. Every fifty or sixty years, however, the bamboo dies. Following large-scale bamboo die-offs in 1983, Chinese wildlife officials found the **emaciated** bodies of 138 pandas. All had starved to death.

The giant panda's plight is **exacerbated** by such predators as the leopard, the Asiatic wild dog, and the brown bear, but the greatest threat comes from human poachers. Although the Chinese government tries to protect the remaining giant pandas by designating penalties of life imprisonment or even death for poachers, the **illicit** trade in skins and live pandas continues. Poachers typically make about $3,000 for each panda skin they sell to a dealer, who sells it for $10,000. One dealer offered two live cubs to a WWF official who was posing as a customer. The asking price was $112,000!

The Chinese government also fights extinction by assisting with the births of panda cubs in captivity. Chinese experts are the leading authorities on panda reproduction, and they provide advice and assistance to zoos trying to breed pandas. Kay and George Schaller, a wife and husband team whose **affinity** with pandas goes back many years, are active with the WWF. They are **ambivalent** about the value of such programs because panda cubs born in captivity rarely survive. The Schallers believe that it may be too late to reverse the **inexorable** decline in the world's panda population. But despite their pessimism, they continue to **proselytize** on the panda's behalf through books, articles, speeches, and television appearances, believing that raising the public's awareness of the panda's plight may help to save it.

In 1992, Ling Ling died, and this marked the **cessation** of Washington National Zoo's breeding program. She had given birth five times, but each cub died from infection within days. Then the San Diego Zoo took up the challenge, and in 1996, it received from China two giant pandas, a female named Bai Yun and a male named Shi Shi. Three years later, Bai Yun gave birth to a baby "no bigger than a stick of butter." Hua Mei, the first panda bred successfully in North America, survived and on August 21, 2000, celebrated her first birthday. By then, she weighed sixty pounds. On February 11, 2004, she was moved to China, where she will spend her days in the famed Wolong Nature Reserve. China requires that all pandas bred through its exchange program be transferred to China after their third birthday.

Hua Mei was a victory for those struggling to preserve the species. However, one small success does not mean that the giant panda's fight for survival has been won. The millions who flock to zoos to observe these rare creatures might reflect on the **poignant** fact that one day, perhaps sooner than we think, they may vanish from the earth.

Answer each of the following questions in the form of a sentence. If a question does not contain a vocabulary word from this lesson's word list, use one in your answer. Use each word only once.

acrimony

affinity

ambivalent

cessation

emaciated

enclave

engender

exacerbate

illicit

indigenous

inexorable

infatuated

insatiable

poignant

proselytize

1. How are leopards, human poachers, and other predators affecting the giant panda's situation?

2. Where can pandas be found in the wild?

3. Why are pandas not found in the wild anywhere in the world outside China?

4. What **poignant** discovery did Chinese game wardens make in 1983?

5. How do we know that the 138 pandas had starved to death?

6. What action did the Chinese government take that it hoped would lead to the **cessation** of poaching?

7. Why do panda poachers continue to operate despite severe penalties?

8. Why do World Wildlife Fund members feel such **acrimony** toward the poachers?

9. Why would it be inaccurate to say that the Schallers are **infatuated** with giant pandas?

10. How many cubs did Ling-Ling and Hsing-Hsing produce over the years?

11. Why do the Schallers not **proselytize** against zoo breeding programs?

12. Why do you think people have such an **affinity** for pandas?

FUN & FASCINATING FACTS

The Latin *ambi-*, "both," combines with the root of the Latin verb *valere*, "to be strong," to form **ambivalent**. A person who is *ambivalent* about something holds two contradictory attitudes toward it but feels equally strongly about them both. A classic case of *ambivalence* is a tale in which a donkey found itself between two piles of hay of equal size. The donkey couldn't decide whether to go right or left and so chose to go left and right simultaneously. Since this option was impossible, the donkey starved to death.

Don't confuse **illicit**, which is an adjective, with *elicit*, which is a verb that means "to bring or draw out." (I managed to *elicit* a statement from him that he had been engaging in *illicit* activities.)

Lesson 6

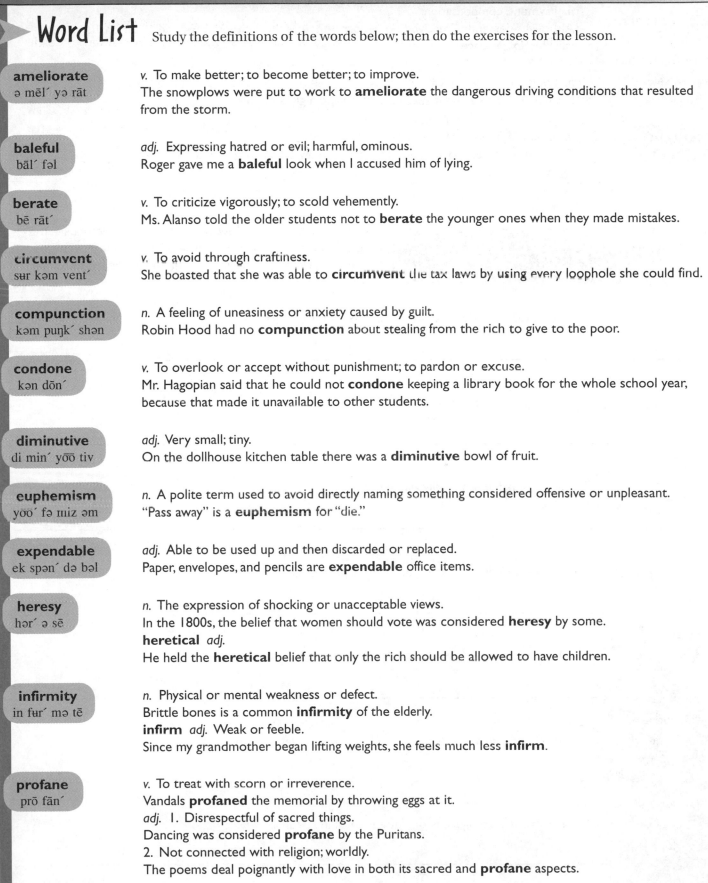

Word List Study the definitions of the words below; then do the exercises for the lesson.

ameliorate
ə mēl´ yə rāt

v. To make better; to become better; to improve.
The snowplows were put to work to **ameliorate** the dangerous driving conditions that resulted from the storm.

baleful
bāl´ fəl

adj. Expressing hatred or evil; harmful, ominous.
Roger gave me a **baleful** look when I accused him of lying.

berate
bē rāt´

v. To criticize vigorously; to scold vehemently.
Ms. Alanso told the older students not to **berate** the younger ones when they made mistakes.

circumvent
sur kəm vent´

v. To avoid through craftiness.
She boasted that she was able to **circumvent** the tax laws by using every loophole she could find.

compunction
kəm puŋk´ shən

n. A feeling of uneasiness or anxiety caused by guilt.
Robin Hood had no **compunction** about stealing from the rich to give to the poor.

condone
kən dōn´

v. To overlook or accept without punishment; to pardon or excuse.
Mr. Hagopian said that he could not **condone** keeping a library book for the whole school year, because that made it unavailable to other students.

diminutive
di min´ yōō tiv

adj. Very small; tiny.
On the dollhouse kitchen table there was a **diminutive** bowl of fruit.

euphemism
yōō´ fə miz əm

n. A polite term used to avoid directly naming something considered offensive or unpleasant.
"Pass away" is a **euphemism** for "die."

expendable
ek spən´ də bəl

adj. Able to be used up and then discarded or replaced.
Paper, envelopes, and pencils are **expendable** office items.

heresy
hər´ ə sē

n. The expression of shocking or unacceptable views.
In the 1800s, the belief that women should vote was considered **heresy** by some.
heretical *adj.*
He held the **heretical** belief that only the rich should be allowed to have children.

infirmity
in fur´ mə tē

n. Physical or mental weakness or defect.
Brittle bones is a common **infirmity** of the elderly.
infirm *adj.* Weak or feeble.
Since my grandmother began lifting weights, she feels much less **infirm**.

profane
prō fān´

v. To treat with scorn or irreverence.
Vandals **profaned** the memorial by throwing eggs at it.
adj. 1. Disrespectful of sacred things.
Dancing was considered **profane** by the Puritans.
2. Not connected with religion; worldly.
The poems deal poignantly with love in both its sacred and **profane** aspects.

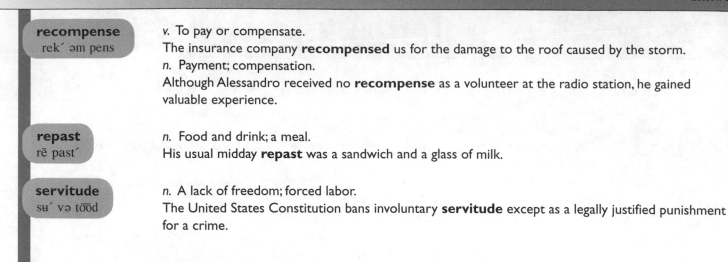

recompense
rek´ əm pens

v. To pay or compensate.
The insurance company **recompensed** us for the damage to the roof caused by the storm.
n. Payment; compensation.
Although Alessandro received no **recompense** as a volunteer at the radio station, he gained valuable experience.

repast
rē past´

n. Food and drink; a meal.
His usual midday **repast** was a sandwich and a glass of milk.

servitude
sʉ´ və tood

n. A lack of freedom; forced labor.
The United States Constitution bans involuntary **servitude** except as a legally justified punishment for a crime.

6A Understanding Meanings

Read the sentences below. If a sentence correctly uses the word in bold, write *C* on the line below it. If a sentence is incorrect, rewrite it so that the vocabulary word in bold is used correctly.

1. To **condone** an action is to disapprove of it strongly.

2. **Compunction** is a feeling of guilt caused by doing wrong.

3. An **infirmity** is a bodily ailment.

4. A **baleful** countenance is one that expresses goodwill.

ameliorate
baleful
berate
circumvent
compunction
condone
diminutive
euphemism
expendable
heresy
infirmity
profane
recompense
repast
servitude

5. To **ameliorate** a condition is to bring about an improvement in it.

6. To **circumvent** a difficulty is to find a way to get around it.

7. A **diminutive** figure is one that is small in stature.

8. **Servitude** is a condition similar to slavery.

9. To **profane** something is to treat it with a lack of respect.

10. **Heresy** is unkind laughter at another person's expense.

11. A **euphemism** is an expression that replaces one considered unacceptable.

12. Something that is **expendable** can be enlarged as needed.

13. To **recompense** someone is to pay that person.

14. To **berate** someone is to scold that person forcefully.

15. A **repast** is a recalling of recent events.

6B Using Words

If the word (or a form of the word) in bold fits in a sentence in the group below it, write the word in the blank. If the word does not fit, leave the space empty.

1. **condone**

   (a) While we don't _____ his behavior, we feel his actions are not our concern.

   (b) How can you condemn bullfighting and, at the same time, _____ fox hunting?

   (c) My best friend came to _____ me after my dog died.

2. expendable

(a) He treats cars as _____ objects to be abandoned when he tires of them.

(b) Because booster rockets are _____ , they are not recovered after they are used.

(c) Since the couple often had guests for dinner, they decided to buy an _____ table.

3. profane

(a) This holy temple is no place for such _____ utterances.

(b) He used to be a priest, but he made a transition to the _____ field of finance.

(c) He would _____ the holy days if he did not fast during them.

4. ameliorate

(a) After the patient's fever broke, her condition began to _____ .

(b) Attempts to _____ the living conditions of the residents have proved ineffective.

(c) You could _____ the soup more quickly by turning up the heat.

5. compunction

(a) She felt little _____ about taking the money, which she felt was rightly hers.

(b) He cheated on the test without _____ .

(c) She directed the crowd with _____ as they exited the burning theater.

6. baleful

(a) Rory suffered _____ injuries when he fell from the ladder.

(b) The letter contained several _____ threats, which I chose to disregard.

(c) His _____ predictions that there would be rioting in the streets fortunately turned out to be false.

7. recompense

(a) You must allow me to _____ you for the trouble you went to on my behalf.

(b) Can you _____ me fifty dollars until I get paid on Friday?

(c) Ten dollars was small _____ for an afternoon's hard work.

8. repast

(a) She knew she was lost when she _____ the same building three times.

(b) The simple _____ consisted of a slice of bread and a piece of cheese.

(c) They lazily _____ on the porch all afternoon.

6C Word Study

Each group of four words below contains two words that are either synonyms or antonyms. Circle these two words; then circle the *S* if they are synonyms, the *A* if they are antonyms.

1. enduring	trusted	adamant	ephemeral	S	A
2. accolade	altercation	quarrel	discovery	S	A
3. endow	reveal	ingratiate	grant	S	A
4. chary	reckless	perverse	poignant	S	A
5. ambivalent	poignant	risky	adamant	S	A
6. adjudicate	engender	curtail	proselytize	S	A
7. gratuitous	alien	insatiable	indigenous	S	A
8. diminuitive	profane	sacred	rampant	S	A
9. recompense	solution	payment	compunction	S	A
10. assiduous	baleful	diminutive	enormous	S	A

6D Images of Words

Circle the letter of each sentence that suggests the numbered bold vocabulary word. In each group, you may circle more than one letter or none at all.

1. **heresy**

   (a) He wore a garish outfit at the picnic.

   (b) The leader of the new party calls for the abolition of Congress.

   (c) Lending money at excessive rates of interest is to be condemned.

2. **servitude**

   (a) Do you see how the prime minister's aides bow to her will?

   (b) She spoke with such conviction that I believed her.

   (c) Russian serfs were bound to their masters and were not free to leave.

3. **infirmity**

   (a) His broken leg kept him from his usual activities for over a month.

   (b) Maya's eyesight is getting worse, but she refuses to wear glasses.

   (c) My great-grandfather is in his nineties, and his mind is starting to wander.

4. **berate**

   (a) Rachel considered the '55 Corvette a better car than the '55 Thunderbird.

   (b) Jorge called Steve an idiot and said he had half a mind to fire him.

   (c) Toni told Ashley, "Please be more careful next time."

5. **compunction**

   (a) Robert claimed that he has been late for work only once in thirty years.

   (b) I admitted that I had no idea how the parts fitted together.

   (c) Lucia couldn't sleep well after she didn't tell her parents that she put a dent in the car.

6. **ameliorate**

   (a) The car runs much better since we switched to premium gasoline.

   (b) The new warden made sure that prisoners would now receive proper medical care.

   (c) The more Marie practiced, the better she got at playing the violin.

7. **circumvent**

   (a) He found a loophole in the law that allowed him to fish without a license.

   (b) By classifying the company's trucks as cars, the importer avoided paying the extra tax on them.

   (c) The moon travels around the earth once every 27.3 days.

8. **diminutive**

   (a) The Mississippi River runs from Minnesota to Louisiana.

   (b) The pictures in Jane's dollhouse were no bigger than postage stamps.

   (c) The huge snowstorm we expected left three feet of snow on the ground.

9. **profane**

   (a) Someone wishing us harm had deliberately poisoned the well water.

   (b) The group complained that modern movies opposed their values.

   (c) The dishonest mechanic overcharged them for his services.

10. **euphemism**

    (a) I'm sorry to say that Ms. Doherty died last week.

    (b) The burial ground is referred to as "The Garden of Heavenly Rest."

    (c) "Excuse me, can you direct me to the ladies' room?"

ameliorate
baleful
berate
circumvent
compunction
condone
diminutive
euphemism
expendable
heresy
infirmity
profane
recompense
repast
servitude

6E Passage Read the passage below; then complete the exercise that follows it.

A Career in the Linen Industry

Elizabeth Bentley was awakened by her mother each morning at 3:00 a.m. Breakfast was a meager **repast**, usually no more than a crust of bread, after which Elizabeth set off on the two-mile walk to the linen factory in England where she worked. Fearful of being late, she often forced herself to run. The factory gates opened at 5:00 a.m., and Mr. Burk, her employer, did not **condone** tardiness. She would be beaten if she were late.

Removing full spools of linen thread from the frames on which they were spun and replacing them with empty ones, Elizabeth worked swiftly under the **baleful** eye of the factory overseer. He would **berate** her if she dawdled and felt no **compunction** about beating her if his threats were not heeded. Hundreds of others worked alongside Elizabeth, and beatings were frequent on the factory floor.

At noon, the frames were shut down for forty minutes. Elizabeth had been working nonstop for seven hours, and she struggled to stay awake to eat her simple midday meal. At 12:40 p.m., the frames were restarted, and Elizabeth worked steadily and without another break until 7:00 p.m. That was during the slack season. During the busy season she worked until 9:00 p.m. After a grueling day's work and her two-mile walk home, Elizabeth, usually too tired to eat, wished only to lay her **diminutive** body on her cot and sleep. She was six years old.

Mr. Burk would not permit employees to **profane** the Sabbath by working on Sundays, so Elizabeth worked only six days a week. She was one of the more fortunate ones, for she had a mother who cared for her, and she received a wage of two shillings a week. Less fortunate were the orphans from the local poorhouse, who were rented out to employers by the poorhouse staff. The orphans received no **recompense** for their labor; their earnings went to the poorhouse. They were called apprentices—a **euphemism** indeed, for they were really slaves, bound to a factory or coal mine for twelve years of **servitude** or until death or **infirmity** cut their working lives short.

After seven years in the linen factory, Elizabeth was in constant pain. Her ankles and knees were so weakened that she could no longer endure the demands imposed by the framing machines. Mr. Burk considered his employees **expendable**, so, at the age of thirteen, she was replaced by a younger and stronger girl. Elizabeth lived at home until her mother died, when Elizabeth was eighteen years old. Unable to support herself, and broken in health, she was placed in the poorhouse.

Although child labor protection laws were passed in 1802, they did little to **ameliorate** conditions for laboring children. Employers found ways to **circumvent** the laws; often parliamentary officials were no help in enforcing them. Many members of Parliament derived their wealth from the profits of cheap child labor, and other members viewed governmental regulation of business as **heretical**.

Fortunately, the government continued to investigate the abuses of children in mines and factories. In 1815, Elizabeth Bentley told her story to a government commission. As a result of her testimony and others like it, the Factory Act, passed in 1833, arranged for a system of factory inspection. The subsequent reports given by the factory inspectors generated public interest, leading to more laws that eventually helped to improve conditions for children in England.

Answer each of the following questions in the form of a sentence. If a question does not contain a vocabulary word from this lesson's word list, use one in your answer. Use each word only once.

1. How much time was allowed for the workers' midday **repast** at Mr. Burk's factory?

2. What **recompense** did Elizabeth receive?

3. Why would it be a **euphemism** to say that children in 1815 were "employed" in mines and factories?

4. Why would Elizabeth's mother probably not have **berated** her for not eating her dinner?

5. What contradiction do you see in Mr. Burk's beliefs and actions?

6. Why was Elizabeth's employment terminated?

7. Why would an eight-hour work day have seemed **heretical** in the era in which Elizabeth was working?

8. Why were factory owners unconcerned by the passing of child labor protection laws in 1802?

9. Why did the British government **condone** child labor?

10. How did the English Factory Act help to improve working conditions for children?

FUN & FASCINATING FACTS

Baleful and *baneful* (Lesson 1) overlap somewhat in meaning, but *baleful* suggests the threat of harm, while *baneful* implies actual harm or destruction. (A *baleful* look from a threatening person might have *baneful* consequences for whomever received such a glance.)

Circumvent is formed from the Latin prefix *circum-*, meaning "around," and the root from the Latin verb *venire*, meaning "to come" or "to go." One way to *circumvent* a difficulty is by going around it rather then confronting it directly. Several other words share this prefix. The *circumference* of the earth is the distance around it at the equator. To *circumnavigate* the earth is to go around it. A *circumlocution* is a roundabout way of saying something rather than a direct statement.

Lesson 7

▶ **Word List** Study the definitions of the words below; then do the exercises for the lesson.

castigate
kas´ ti gāt

v. To punish by criticizing sharply; to berate.
Our former principal used to **castigate** students in public; Ms. Abrosino would never do that.

colloquial
kə lō´ kwē əl

adj. Characterized by informal language.
Most of the lecturers were formal and boring, but the last one was more engaging and lively because of her **colloquial** speech.
colloquialism *n.*
"Y'all come back" is known as a Southern **colloquialism**.

epitaph
ep´ ə taf

n. The words carved on a tombstone in memory of the deceased.
The gravestone had no **epitaph**, just the name Al Cott and the dates 1813–1865.

exodus
ek´ sə dəs

n. A mass departure.
Poverty and political misrule caused the **exodus** of Haitians from their homeland to the United States.

inter
in tʉr´

v. To put in a grave; to bury.
Soon after the funeral, his body was **interred** in its grave.
interment *n.*
Before the **interment**, they placed flowers on the coffin.

lacerate
las´ ər āt

v. To tear or cut roughly.
My legs were **lacerated** by the rocks as we climbed to the peak.
laceration *n.*
The animal trainer suffered a minor **laceration** of his arm when a rambunctious lion hit him with its paw.

largesse
lär jes´

n. The act of giving generously; gifts.
After donating a large amount of money to a homeless shelter, the man received an award in recognition of his **largesse**.

obituary
ō bich´ ōō er ē

n. A notice of someone's death, such as in a newspaper, usually with a brief summary of that person's life.
I didn't know she'd died until I saw her **obituary** in the local paper.

omnivorous
äm niv´ ər əs

adj. 1. Eating all kinds of food, including both animal and vegetable food.
Even though some people are vegetarians, the human species is classified as **omnivorous**, because humans may eat both animal and vegetable products.
2. Taking in everything available.
They were **omnivorous** collectors of everything from rare books to old theatrical posters.

permeate
pʉr´ mē āt

v. To spread throughout; to pass through.
The smell of garlic **permeated** the kitchen.

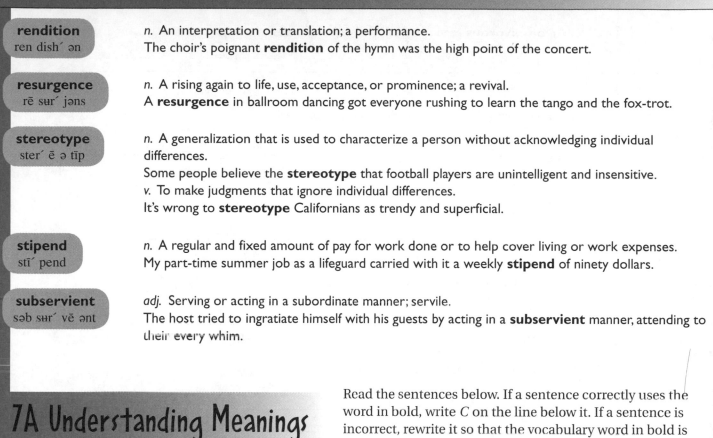

rendition
ren dish´ ən

n. An interpretation or translation; a performance.
The choir's poignant **rendition** of the hymn was the high point of the concert.

resurgence
rē sur´ jəns

n. A rising again to life, use, acceptance, or prominence; a revival.
A **resurgence** in ballroom dancing got everyone rushing to learn the tango and the fox-trot.

stereotype
ster´ ē ə tīp

n. A generalization that is used to characterize a person without acknowledging individual differences.
Some people believe the **stereotype** that football players are unintelligent and insensitive.
v. To make judgments that ignore individual differences.
It's wrong to **stereotype** Californians as trendy and superficial.

stipend
stī´ pend

n. A regular and fixed amount of pay for work done or to help cover living or work expenses.
My part-time summer job as a lifeguard carried with it a weekly **stipend** of ninety dollars.

subservient
səb sur´ vē ənt

adj. Serving or acting in a subordinate manner; servile.
The host tried to ingratiate himself with his guests by acting in a **subservient** manner, attending to their every whim.

7A Understanding Meanings

Read the sentences below. If a sentence correctly uses the word in bold, write *C* on the line below it. If a sentence is incorrect, rewrite it so that the vocabulary word in bold is used correctly.

1. A **rendition** of a song is a performance of it.

2. **Largesse** is the maximum size available.

3. An **obituary** is a brief statement reporting a person's death.

4. A **subservient** person is one inclined to submit to others.

5. A smell that **permeates** a building spreads throughout it.

6. An **omnivorous** reader is one who reads all types of books.

7. A **laceration** is an injury made by cutting or tearing.

8. An **interment** is a burial.

9. To **stereotype** people is to disregard differences among individuals.

10. An **exodus** is a route between two places.

11. An **epitaph** is a term of abuse.

12. If there is a **resurgence** of a sport, then that sport is making a comeback.

13. To **castigate** someone is to put that person down.

14. A **stipend** is a salary for services rendered.

15. A **colloquialism** is a serious or formal discussion.

castigate
colloquial
epitaph
exodus
inter
lacerate
largesse
obituary
omnivorous
permeate
rendition
resurgence
stereotype
stipend
subservient

7B Using Words

If the word (or a form of the word) in bold fits in a sentence in the group below it, write the word in the blank. If the word does not fit, leave the space empty.

1. **subservient**

   (a) He could treat his boss with respect without being so _____ .

   (b) A private's rank is _____ to that of a general in the army.

   (c) The Speaker of the House replaced his independent and outspoken aide for someone more _____ .

2. **obituary**

   (a) His _____ stated merely that he had died after a brief illness.

   (b) On the anniversary of the poet's death, a crowd gathered to hear a reading of her _____ and several readings of her poems.

   (c) The _____ on the old tombstone read simply "Here lieth Caleb Crabbe."

3. **colloquial**

   (a) Nothing of great importance was discussed at these _____ meetings.

   (b) "You ain't seen nothin' yet" is a _____ expression.

   (c) His way of dressing was too _____ for the formal restaurant.

4. **interment**

   (a) The _____ at the Grove Hill Cemetery took place after a brief memorial service.

   (b) She took a summer _____ at a law office.

   (c) The practices of some religions encourage _____ instead of cremation.

5. **permeate**

   (a) A distrust of government began to _____ the electorate after the politicians broke their promises.

   (b) A smell of fried onions always seemed to _____ the apartment building.

   (c) The dense clay soil does not allow the rain to _____ below the surface.

6. **exodus**

   (a) As soon as the meeting ended, there was a rush for the _____ .

   (b) The Great Famine caused an _____ of people from Ireland in the 1840s.

   (c) As President Polk made his stately _____ , he turned in the doorway and bowed to us.

7. lacerate

(a) The Bulldogs _____ the home team by a score of 87 points to 14.

(b) Thorny twigs _____ our bare legs as we raced through the underbrush.

(c) Shells were wet and _____ in the sun.

8. omnivorous

(a) Pigs and humans are both _____ creatures.

(b) An _____ reader, he had an extremely well-stocked library.

(c) She gave an _____ sigh as the plates of food were brought in.

7C Word Study

Complete the analogies by selecting the pair of words whose relationship most resembles the relationship of the pair in capital letters. Circle the letter in front of the pair you choose.

1. RECOMPENSE : STIPEND ::
   - (a) undermine : confidence
   - (b) cultivate : plant
   - (c) reject : offer
   - (d) endow : gift

2. EXACERBATE : AMELIORATE ::
   - (a) judge : adjudicate
   - (b) fascinate : mesmerize
   - (c) malign : adulate
   - (d) curtail : reduce

3. FOND : INFATUATED ::
   - (a) hostile : baleful
   - (b) huge : diminutive
   - (c) haughty : subservient
   - (d) legal : illicit

4. COLLOQUIAL : FORMAL ::
   - (a) sad : poignant
   - (b) carnivorous : omnivorous
   - (c) local : indigenous
   - (d) garish : elegant

5. THIN : EMACIATED ::
   - (a) hungry : insatiable
   - (b) free : gratuitous
   - (c) real : illusory
   - (d) genuine : spurious

6. SERVITUDE : FREEDOM ::
   - (a) countenance : face
   - (b) infirmity : strength
   - (c) equilibrium : balance
   - (d) indignity : insult

7. ESPIONAGE : SPY ::
   - (a) vision : eye
   - (b) tree : oak
   - (c) surgery : doctor
   - (d) clique : outsider

castigate
colloquial
epitaph
exodus
inter
lacerate
largesse
obituary
omnivorous
permeate
rendition
resurgence
stereotype
stipend
subservient

8. INSTRUCTION : TUTELAGE ::

    (a) praise : accolade   (c) death : obituary

    (b) rendition : song   (d) harmony : rancor

9. INCARCERATE : IMPRISON ::

    (a) liberate : free   (c) permeate : space

    (b) castigate : blunder   (d) elevate : pantheon

10. DECLINE : RESURGENCE ::

    (a) exodus : departure   (c) indignity : accolade

    (b) repast : meal   (d) affinity : attraction

7D Images of Words

Circle the letter of each sentence that suggests the numbered bold vocabulary word. In each group, you may circle more than one letter or none at all.

1. **largesse**

    (a) Last night's blizzard resulted in almost two feet of snow in the valley.

    (b) Last year I deposited nearly two thousand dollars into my savings account.

    (c) Niles depended on the generosity of his uncle for his college expenses.

2. **castigate**

    (a) Catherine appreciates the invitation to your party, but she'd rather not go.

    (b) She called her insensitive, undependable, and irresponsible.

    (c) They never could see eye-to-eye and finally just decided to part ways.

3. **exodus**

    (a) Millions of Americans moved from the cities to the suburbs in the 1950s.

    (b) The bus for New Orleans leaves in five minutes.

    (c) The only way off the island was by boat, and hundreds flocked to the first ship ashore.

4. **stipend**

    (a) The library position pays a small salary of five thousand dollars a year.

    (b) There's a fifty-dollar reward for the person who finds the missing dog.

    (c) The scholarship allowed for a certain amount of money to be used for living expenses.

5. **rendition**

    (a) The movie *Clueless* is a modern interpretation of Jane Austen's novel *Emma*.

    (b) Many have played Othello but Laurence Olivier's performance is considered exceptionally powerful.

    (c) She placed second in the spelling bee.

6. **omnivorous**

   (a) The tiger let out a deafening roar.

   (b) The emperor was known as an all-powerful ruler.

   (c) He had the look of someone who hadn't eaten in days.

7. **colloquial**

   (a) When she realized her sons had entered her in the singing contest, she complained, "You got me in a real pickle, boys."

   (b) They loved working on the quilt together every Saturday afternoon.

   (c) The note ended, "I have the Honor to be, Sir, Your Most Obedient Servant."

8. **resurgence**

   (a) Bell-bottoms have made a comeback.

   (b) After years of neglect, folk music is becoming popular again.

   (c) The dramatic increase in tuberculosis cases concerns health officials.

9. **lacerate**

   (a) He got those nicks and cuts on his leg when he went through the hole in the fence.

   (b) The baseball player hit the ball with such force that you could hear the hit down the street.

   (c) The bubbles floated in the breeze and then popped, one by one.

10. **stereotype**

   (a) By looking through both lenses, you see a three-dimensional image.

   (b) She played her CDs so loudly, the police came to tell her to turn her music down.

   (c) Those glasses and old-fashioned clothes make him look like an absentminded professor.

castigate
colloquial
epitaph
exodus
inter
lacerate
largesse
obituary
omnivorous
permeate
rendition
resurgence
stereotype
stipend
subservient

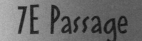 **7E Passage**   Read the passage below; then complete the exercise that follows it.

A Genius of the South

When Zora Neale Hurston was born in Eatonville, Florida, in 1891, her hometown was the first and only all-black town in the United States. Even as a child, Hurston had a strong, independent spirit and found it hard to believe that her color could interfere with her dreams. But because Hurston's father knew that blacks were often expected to be **subservient** to whites and were **castigated** if they failed to kowtow, he worried that she would get into trouble for not knowing her place. But her mother always encouraged her to "jump at de sun."

Hurston was a big dreamer with a vivid and active imagination that was fostered by listening to the "lying" sessions that took place at the local store. Whenever Hurston could, she would go to the store, where men would gather and entertain each other with tall tales—the taller the better.

In addition to listening to stories, Hurston was an **omnivorous** reader, but she especially loved reading myths and fairy tales. Once, two women from Minnesota came to visit Hurston's school. They were so impressed when Hurston read a Greek myth to them that they gave her several gifts, including a book of fairy tales. After they left, their **largesse** continued when they sent Hurston a huge box of books of more fairy tales, novels, and myths, which she loved most of all.

After Hurston's mother died in 1904, she lived with relatives who expected her to work instead of going to school. It was not until she began to live on her own in the city of Baltimore that she continued her education.

Hurston was determined to graduate from high school. She worked during the day at various odd jobs to pay her bills and went to school in the evening. In 1918, Hurston moved to Washington, D.C., where she attended Howard University, and later to New York, where she attended Columbia University in 1925.

While at Columbia, Hurston studied anthropology, the study of human origins, social relations, and culture. She concentrated on folklore and was awarded a **stipend** of $200 a month to travel through the South, the Caribbean, and British Honduras (now Belize) to collect folklore and learn about local customs, such as voodoo. In 1935, Hurston was the first African American to publish a collection of African American folklore when she published *Mules and Men*.

Hurston's move to New York in 1925 took place during an **exodus** from the South called the Great Migration. More than a million blacks moved to the North during the 1910s and 1920s. During this time, a large community of black writers, musicians, and other artists gathered to share and explore their talents and to help each other grow as artists in a movement known as the Harlem Renaissance. Hurston became heavily involved in this movement and wrote novels, poems, short stories, plays, journal articles, and an autobiography, *Dust Tracks on a Road*.

Hurston's love of her heritage **permeates** her work, and in her writings she uses the **colloquial** speech of her upbringing in the South. Hurston's writing met with controversy because some people felt that she was advancing the **stereotype** that blacks were poorly educated people incapable of speaking correct English. But she felt that her **rendition** of Southern black life was not only accurate, it expressed a colorful and fanciful use of language of which, she felt, blacks could be proud.

After the Harlem Renaissance, the popularity of Hurston's work began to fade, and publishers lost interest in her work. Her death in 1960 was publicly overlooked except for a small **obituary** in *Time* magazine.

Pulitzer Prize–winning author Alice Walker was extremely disturbed that Hurston was not better recognized for her greatness as an artist while she was alive. When Walker went to visit Hurston's unmarked grave in 1973, she was offended to find an unkempt graveyard with a tangle of overgrown weeds and shoulder-high bushes. Thorns **lacerated** Walker's bare legs as she made her way through the abandoned graveyard, searching for the grave where Hurston's body had been **interred** thirteen years before. Once she found the grave, she ordered a handsome gray stone to mark the grave site. The **epitaph** reads "Zora Neale Hurston, A Genius of the South, Novelist, Folklorist, Anthropologist."

It is largely due to Alice Walker's efforts that there has been a **resurgence** of interest in Hurston's writings, and all her books are back in print. Her best-known work, *Their Eyes Were Watching God*, is now recognized as a classic.

Answer each of the following questions in the form of a sentence. If a question does not contain a vocabulary word from this lesson's word list, use one in your answer. Use each word only once.

1. Is it accurate to say that Hurston only read myths as a child?

2. Why did Hurston's father worry about her when she was a girl?

3. What did Hurston do with the $200 **stipend** that she was awarded?

4. When did Hurston move to New York?

5. How does the author of the passage first suggest that Hurston appreciated the Southern black culture in which she grew up?

6. Why was Hurston's writing met with controversy?

7. How might those who knew her have learned of Hurston's death?

8. What was Walker looking for in 1973?

9. What did Walker do to acknowledge Hurston's contribution to literature and anthropology?

10. What has been the result of Walker's interest in Hurston's work?

FUN & FASCINATING FACTS

Two Greek words, *exo*, meaning "out," and *hodos*, meaning "way," combine to form **exodus**. *Exodus* is also the name of the second book of the Old Testament, which tells of the Jews' flight from slavery in Egypt.

The word **inter** is derived from the Latin word *terra*, which means "earth" or "ground." Several other words use the same root. A *subterranean* stream is one lying under the ground. The *Mediterranean* Sea was once thought to be at the center of the earth by the Romans and ancient Greeks. *Terrain* refers to the character of the ground, whether it's hilly or flat, for example. *Territory* refers to regions of land.

The Latin prefix *omni-* means "all" and is found in several English words. To be *omnipotent* is to be all-powerful. To be *omniscient* is to be all-knowing. To be *omnipresent* is to be present everywhere. The word *bus* is a shortened form of *omnibus*, which originally referred to a vehicle that was available for all who wished to use it.

The Latin verb *vorare*, meaning "to devour," forms the root of several English words. An *herbivorous* animal eats only plants. A *carnivorous* animal eats only meat. A *voracious* appetite is one not easily satisfied.

By combining the Latin prefix *omni-*, meaning "all," with the Latin root *vorare*, meaning "to devour," we form the word **omnivorous**. An omnivorous creature is one that eats products from both animals and plants.

Lesson 8

Word List
Study the definitions of the words below; then do the exercises for the lesson.

adjacent
ə jā´ sənt

adj. Near or next to; adjoining.
The two couples requested **adjacent** rooms when they checked into the hotel.

beset
bē set´

v. 1. To surround or to attack repeatedly.
Mosquitoes **beset** the campers as soon as they entered the woods.
2. To trouble or weigh down.
Some veterans of the Gulf War were **beset** by a variety of ailments after they returned home.

cede
sēd

v. To give up or transfer, especially by treaty or formal agreement.
France **ceded** vast territories to the United States as part of the 1803 Louisiana Purchase.

circuitous
sər kyōō´ i təs

adj. Roundabout; indirect.
Before the Panama Canal was completed in 1914, ships had to travel a **circuitous** route around South America.

desultory
des´ əl tô ē

adj. Proceeding or carried out in an aimless or random way.
After my best friend moved away, our phone conversations became more and more **desultory**.

galvanize
gal´ və nīz

v. To excite or arouse action.
The discovery of gold in California **galvanized** Easterners to go West to seek their fortunes.

implement
im´ plə mənt

n. A tool or instrument.
My father keeps his woodworking **implements** in the tool shed.
v. To carry out.
The governor **implemented** his plan for health care reform as soon as he took office.

inconseqential
in kän sə kwen´ shəl

adj. Lacking importance or worth; unable to make an impact; trivial.
The issue of cafeteria hours seemed so **inconsequential** that I didn't bother to raise it at the meeting.

magnitude
mag´ nə tōod

n. Greatness of size, power, or influence.
The **magnitude** of the success of her book thrilled the author.

materialize
mə tir´ ē əl īz

v. 1. To become real or actual.
When offers of financial support did not **materialize**, I was forced to abandon the research project.
2. To appear in physical form, especially suddenly.
The trapped miners were about to abandon hope when the rescue crew **materialized**.

muster
mus´ tər

n. A gathering, usually of military forces.
The evening **muster** of the troops was held at 6:00 p.m. sharp.
v. To summon or call forth; to gather.
Sam wanted to ask for a raise but couldn't **muster** the courage to ask his boss.

| **prohibitive** | *adj.* Serving to restrain action or discourage use of. |
| prō hib´ ə tiv | Many students couldn't attend the concert because the ticket prices were **prohibitive**. |

reminisce	*v.* To think or talk about one's past.
rem ə nis´	My grandparents like to **reminisce** about when they were our age.
	reminiscence *n.* The act of remembering; a recollection.
	Reminiscences often blur with time.
	reminiscent *adj.* Suggestive of something else.
	The land where the miners settled was **reminiscent** of the Welsh valleys they had left behind.

| **vanguard** | *n.* The leading or forward position in a movement. |
| van´ gärd | Andy Warhol was in the **vanguard** of the pop art movement. |

visionary	*n.* A person who is given to ideas that are not currently realistic; a dreamer.
vish´ ən er ē	Nelson Mandela is a South African **visionary** who has made ending apartheid his life's work.
	adj. Able to see what might be accomplished in the future.
	President Kennedy had the **visionary** goal of landing people on the moon.

8A Understanding Meanings

Read the sentences below. If a sentence correctly uses the word in bold, write *C* on the line below it. If a sentence is incorrect, rewrite it so that the vocabulary word in bold is used correctly.

1. Someone who is **galvanized** is stimulated to do something.

_____

2. The **magnitude** of something is its size or extent.

_____

3. To be **beset** with something is to be burdened by it.

_____

4. Two things that are **adjacent** are side-by-side.

_____

5. A **desultory** survey is one with disturbing results.

_____

6. A **muster** is a group that is brought together.

7. Something that **materializes** comes into view.

8. To **cede** a point is to yield it.

9. An **inconsequential** action is one with unforeseen consequences.

10. A **vanguard** is a device that protects against damage.

11. **Prohibitive** measures are those that dissuade or hinder.

12. Something that is **reminiscent** of the past reminds you of it.

13. **Circuitous** language is not direct or straightforward.

14. An **implement** is a change of plan or direction.

15. A **visionary** goal is one that is doomed to failure.

adjacent
beset
cede
circuitous
desultory
galvanize
implement
inconsequential
magnitude
materialize
muster
prohibitive
reminisce
vanguard
visionary

8B Using Words

If the word (or a form of the word) in bold fits in a sentence in the group below it, write the word in the blank. If the word does not fit, leave the space empty.

1. **reminisce**

   (a) A high school reunion is a perfect opportunity to _____ about the old days.

   (b) I do _____ meeting him but can't remember where or when it was.

   (c) Sitting around a wood fire on a camping trip can be a time to _____ .

2. **visionary**

   (a) Bill Gates is a _____ who saw the great future of personal computers.

   (b) Wernher von Braun was a rocket engineer who lived to see his _____ goal of space travel realized.

   (c) A _____ look came into her eyes when she spoke of the future.

3. **adjacent**

   (a) Since the two yards are _____ , they can be combined into one large yard.

   (b) The town square and _____ streets are closed off for the parade.

   (c) My younger brother Ted is the most _____ to me in age.

4. **beset**

   (a) She was quite unaware of the problems that can _____ new businesses.

   (b) Earlier this year we were _____ by financial difficulties until my mother got a promotion at work.

   (c) I told her she could _____ her mind at rest for we would help her find an apartment.

5. **materialize**

   (a) A figure seemed to _____ out of thin air.

   (b) The new job I had set my hopes on failed to _____ .

   (c) Rumpelstiltskin was able to take straw and _____ it into gold.

6. **magnitude**

   (a) The _____ of the crime calls for the most severe sentence.

   (b) Scientists measure the _____ of an earthquake on the Richter scale.

   (c) The _____ of her literary output is impressive by any standard.

7. **galvanize**

   (a) The delivery of the pizza _____ my parents into action; they had the table set in two minutes.

   (b) A loud knock on the door _____ the dogs into furious leaping and barking.

   (c) She stared at the stranger as though _____ by his piercing eyes.

8. **implement**

(a) The spade is perhaps the most common gardening _____ .

(b) Congress has an obligation to _____ the will of the people.

(c) He wondered why she was trying to make an _____ out of him.

8C Word Study

Change each of the nouns below into an adjective by changing, adding, or dropping the suffix. Write the word in the space provided.

Noun	Adjective
1. reminiscence	_____
2. extrovert	_____
3. infirmity	_____
4. infamy	_____
5. perversity	_____

Change each of the verbs below into a noun by changing, adding, or dropping the suffix. Write the word in the space provided.

Verb	Noun
6. lacerate	_____
7. inter	_____
8. discriminate	_____
9. perpetrate	_____
10. adulate	_____

Change each of the adjectives below into a noun by changing, adding, or dropping the suffix. Write the word in the space provided.

Adjective	Noun
11. acrimonious	_____
12. ambivalent	_____
13. infatuated	_____
14. heretical	_____
15. colloquial	_____

adjacent

beset

cede

circuitous

desultory

galvanize

implement

inconsequential

magnitude

materialize

muster

prohibitive

reminisce

vanguard

visionary

8D Images of Words

Circle the letter of each sentence that suggests the numbered bold vocabulary word. In each group, you may circle more than one letter or none at all.

1. **circuitous**

   (a) We traveled from New York to Seattle via San Antonio and Los Angeles.

   (b) The straight-line distance between Boston and Chicago is about 850 miles.

   (c) Even though the river is 90 miles in length, it's so winding that it ends only 20 miles from its source.

2. **implement**

   (a) Once the plan is decided upon, it is up to you to make it work.

   (b) You need a sledgehammer to split that wood.

   (c) The awning provided shade as well as protection from occasional rain showers.

3. **muster**

   (a) It's amazing the way the sheep dogs keep the sheep in a group.

   (b) Although Todd had promised fifty recruits would show up, only twenty came.

   (c) The on-duty police officers report at 11:00 p.m. to receive instructions for the night shift.

4. **vanguard**

   (a) Claude Monet was one of the first artists to paint in the Impressionist style.

   (b) Because her last name was Abbott, Jill was always first in line at school.

   (c) Stephen Jay Gould was a scientist in the forefront of evolution theory.

5. **cede**

   (a) Nine southern states withdrew from the Union to form the Confederacy.

   (b) After nearly three years of fighting, China gave up the island of Hong Kong to Britain in 1842.

   (c) Once he lost his rook, John realized that he would probably lose the chess game, so he gave up, saying, "Okay, you win."

6. **inconsequential**

   (a) The new regulation will have no noticeable effect on United States citizens.

   (b) She is so rich that the price of that car wouldn't even make a dent in her bank account.

   (c) No one paid the slightest attention to his objections.

7. **visionary**

   (a) Grandmother Kelly is 87 and can still read fine print without glasses.

   (b) Ferdinand de Lesseps's dream of building a canal at Suez was realized in the 1860s.

   (c) Jason fell asleep that night, hoping that the tooth fairy would visit.

8. **reminisce**

(a) Next year we plan to go on a cruise from Los Angeles to Acapulco.

(b) Abraham Lincoln was born in Hardin County, Kentucky, in 1809.

(c) They talked about the treehouse they used to play in as children.

9. **desultory**

(a) The conversation was aimless and marked by long periods of silence.

(b) It took Jamie an hour to finish a task that would normally take her ten minutes to complete.

(c) He read every article in that magazine before putting it down.

10. **prohibitive**

(a) We knew that we were not allowed inside the principal's office.

(b) Experts warn that heating oil could triple in price over the winter months.

(c) The cost of launching a nuclear attack was too great for either side.

8E Passage

Read the passage below; then complete the exercise that follows it.

North to Alaska

The fiftieth anniversary of the completion of the Alaska Highway was celebrated in 1992 at more than 200 locations along its 1,442-mile stretch. Many of those who had helped to build the highway took part in the celebration. Although the construction was **beset** by almost insurmountable difficulties, the highway was completed in less than nine months. It follows a **circuitous** path from Dawson Creek, British Columbia, to Delta Junction, Alaska, and today is traveled by more than 40,000 vehicles every year.

The United States bought Alaska from Russia in 1867 for $7.2 million, the equivalent of eleven cents an acre. Unfortunately for the United States, Alaska could only be reached from the rest of the country by boat.

adjacent
beset
cede
circuitous
desultory
galvanize
implement
inconsequential
magnitude
materialize
muster
prohibitive
reminisce
vanguard
visionary

A few **visionaries** dreamed of building a highway to connect Alaska with the rest of the United States, and a few **desultory** attempts were made and quickly abandoned. The **magnitude** of the task was daunting; most of the highway would have to cross Canada. But Canada was unwilling to **cede** control of any of its territory and the United States refused to proceed without unrestricted access. In addition, constructing the highway over Canada's soft, swamp-like land would be difficult. This complication would add to the cost of the project, making the expense **prohibitive**. Finally, although the people of Alaska would gain from it, the benefits to the southern states were expected to be **inconsequential**.

The United States government's hesitation to go forward with the project changed on December 7, 1941, when the country found itself at war with Japan. In June of the following year, Japanese planes attacked the U.S. naval base at Dutch Harbor, a village on one of the Aleutian Islands, which are **adjacent** to Alaska. The Japanese also occupied another two of these islands. If mainland Alaska were invaded by sea, the United States would have no way of protecting it without a highway.

The U.S. government was **galvanized** into action. The Army Corps of Engineers was given seven days to draw up a plan to build the Alaska Highway. Canada, equally fearful of a Japanese invasion, supported the effort, and the plan was **implemented** without delay.

Ten thousand troops were **mustered** for the task, together with a similar number of civilian workers. The speed with which the project proceeded astonished the inhabitants who lived in scattered settlements along its length. In the **vanguard** were the survey crews who laid out the route, with all of its many twists and turns. Construction workers followed, chopping down trees and laying them crosswise on top of the soft land to prevent the road from sinking.

Reminiscing after fifty years, workers agreed that the experience with the project was thoroughly unpleasant. They remembered the mosquitoes most vividly. During the summer months the insects seemed to **materialize** out of nowhere, wherever skin was exposed. Workers wore nets on their heads as protection, but each time they lifted them to eat, a dozen or more mosquitoes would slip through. As winter approached and the project neared completion, bitter cold became the enemy. Temperatures plummeted to seventy degrees below zero, and fires were lit under trucks at night to make sure they started in the morning.

The road was completed on schedule and was officially opened on November 20, 1942. Japan, aware that troops and supplies could now be rushed to Alaska's defense, made no attempt to occupy it. The original dirt road is now paved over 90 percent of its length, and over the years, tens of thousands of people have traveled it.

Answer each of the following questions in the form of a sentence. If a question does not contain a vocabulary word from this lesson's word list, use one in your answer. Use each word only once.

1. Explain why previous attempts to build the highway were never **implemented**.

2. Why would it be inaccurate to say that earlier attempts to construct the highway were focused and efficient?

3. How did Canada feel about **ceding** control of its territory to the United States?

4. What effect did the attack on Dutch Harbor have on the U.S. government?

5. Why do you think Japanese troops occupied some of the Aleutian Islands?

6. When did the cost of the project no longer seem **prohibitive**?

7. What crucial job did the survey crews perform?

8. Name three difficulties that **beset** the project.

9. Explain why the distance from Dawson Creek to Delta Junction is longer by road than by air.

10. What did the builders of the highway talk about at their reunion?

FUN & FASCINATING FACTS

Luigi Galvani (1737–1798) was an Italian physician who performed experiments on frogs' legs in an attempt to prove that muscles generate electricity when they contract. It turned out that the opposite is true (muscles contract when stimulated with an electric current), but because of Galvani's work, several words that relate to electricity have been derived from his name. A *galvanometer* is an instrument that measures small electric currents. A *galvanic* cell is an electric battery cell that cannot be recharged. *Galvanized* iron is sheet metal coated with zinc through an electrical process. To **galvanize** a muscle is to stimulate or shock it with an electric current. Later, the definition of *galvanize* broadened to mean "to arouse to awareness or action."

In astronomy, **magnitude** refers to the relative brightness of a star. The system for ranking stars by how bright they appear from Earth was developed by the astronomer Ptolemy in the second century. He categorized stars into six magnitudes. The brightest stars were classified as the first magnitude and the faintest ones were classified as the sixth magnitude. This system is still used today, although it has been adjusted to include brighter stars that have negative magnitudes. For instance, Sirius, the brightest star outside of our solar system, has a magnitude of -1.6, and the Sun—which is 10 billion times brighter than Sirius—has a magnitude of -26.7.

Old French was the language of France between the years 900 and 1500, approximately. *Avaunt garde* is an Old French phrase referring to a guard in an advanced position. The phrase has passed into English as **vanguard**. It also survives in the expression *avant-garde*. The avant-garde is a group in society that is active in developing new forms and techniques, especially in the arts.

Review for Lessons 5–8

Hidden Message In the boxes provided, write the words from Lessons 5 through 8 that are missing in each of the sentences below. The number following each sentence gives the word list from which the missing word must be taken. When the exercise is finished, the shaded boxes will spell out a piece of wisdom from Charles F. Kettering, automobile executive, engineer, and inventor, and cofounder of the Sloan-Kettering Cancer Institute.

1. _____ of heartbeat is a sign of death. (5)

2. Her _____ feet fitted inside size 2 shoes. (6)

3. Their starvation diet had left them _____ . (5)

4. Police broke up the _____ gambling operation. (5)

5. His _____ countenance was proof of his anger. (6)

6. There was an _____ of birds migrating south. (7)

7. I've been _____ with many problems this year. (8)

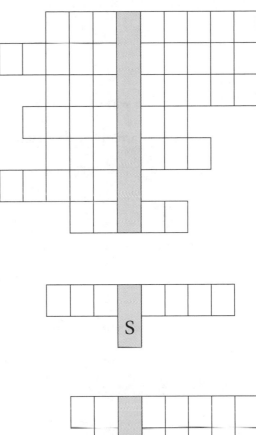

8. A peace offering ended the _____ between them. (5)

9. These false reports _____ mistrust in the people. (5)

10. She would _____ the puppy for tearing up the furniture. (6)

11. It was _____ to question the pope's decision. (6)

12. They _____ their dead in shallow graves. (7)

13. Anna's _____ of the song drew great applause. (7)

14. The encyclopedia was _____ because it was so outdated. (6)

15. Maple trees are _____ to New England. (5)

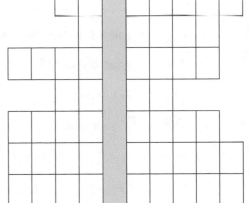

16. "Let go" is a _____ for "fired." (6)

17. The herb garden is _____ to the patio. (8)

18. Unfortunately, the company president will _____ his employees if they disagree with him. (7)

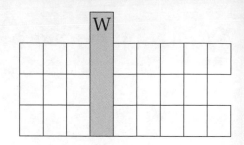

19. R. Goddard was the _____ who pioneered rocketry. (8)

20. I was unaware of her death until I read her _____ . (7)

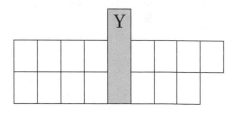

21. This discovery will _____ research toward finding out more about black holes. (8)

22. The poet's _____ with nature is clearly expressed. (5)

23. His _____ desire to dominate led to his downfall. (5)

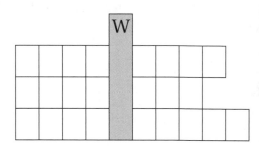

24. I'm _____ about getting another dog. (5)

25. The _____ simply said, "Beloved husband of Julie." (7)

26. They receive a small _____ while in training. (7)

27. The _____ poem left me feeling very sad. (5)

28. I cannot _____ your failure to report for work. (6)

29. When did France _____ Quebec to England? (8)

30. My aunt and uncle's _____ enabled me to go to college. (7)

31. A magnificent _____ was laid before the diners. (6)

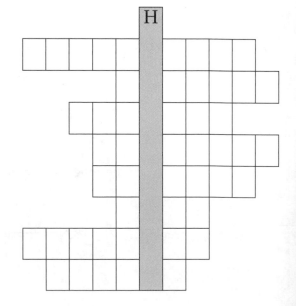

32. Kevin worked hard to _____ the condition of his garden after it was damaged in a storm. (6)

33. We can _____ plenty of support for the project. (8)

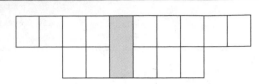

34. Wonderful scents _____ the flower shop. (7)

35. He showed no _____ in cheating his neighbor. (6)

36. Such _____ efforts were bound to fail. (8)

37. A slight _____ kept her in bed for a few days. (6)

38. The rebels occupied a small _____ in the east. (5)

39. Corinna was known for being in the _____ of her field. (8)

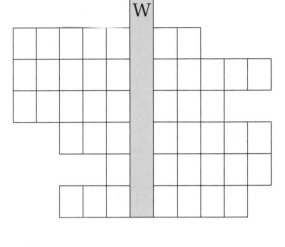

40. Using _____ language in church is shocking. (6)

41. The _____ of the storm surprised everyone. (8)

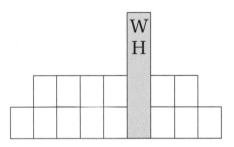

42. The _____ progress of the mudslide forced them to abandon their house before it slid down a hill. (5)

43. There were many twists and turns along the _____ road. (8)

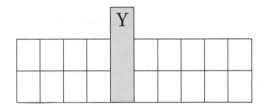

44. The 1990s saw a _____ in 1970s fashions. (7)

45. Strong sunlight will _____ his skin condition. (5)

46. Those captured were held in _____ until they were rescued. (6)

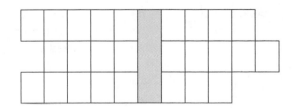

Lesson 9

> ## Word List
Study the definitions of the words below; then do the exercises for the lesson.

cautionary
kô´ shə ner ē

adj. Offering or serving as a warning.
Aesop's fables are **cautionary** tales; their morals are intended to teach lessons.

constrain
kən strān´

v. To confine, inhibit, or hold back by force or necessity.
Abraham Lincoln was not **constrained** by his humble birth.
constraint *n.* A restriction or limitation.
After the curriculum reform went into effect, teachers could select materials without **constraint**.

flotilla
flō til´ ə

n. A fleet of boats or small ships.
A **flotilla** of tall ships sailed into Baltimore's Inner Harbor as part of the city's celebrations.

gossamer
gäs´ ə mər

n. 1. Thin, sheer fabric resembling gauze.
Her veil was **gossamer** and revealed her radiant face.
2. A fine, filmy substance made of strands of cobweb.
The dewy grass held moist bits of **gossamer**.
adj. As light and delicate as a cobweb.
The bride lifted her **gossamer** veil and she and the groom embraced.

ignominious
ig nə min´ ē əs

adj. Marked by, deserving, or causing shame or disgrace.
The off-key singer made an **ignominious** exit from the stage, foregoing the encore he had planned.

incur
in kur´

v. To bring upon oneself something undesirable, such as a debt.
When she voted against giving out raises this year, the supervisor further **incurred** the hostility of her disgruntled workers.

liquidate
lik´ wi dāt

v. 1. To settle the affairs of a business; to convert into cash.
They **liquidated** their assets by selling almost all of their possessions, and used the proceeds to pay their debts.
2. To get rid of; to kill or destroy.
Tens of thousands of Guatemalan peasants were **liquidated** by the military dictatorship in the late 1970s and early 1980s.

magnate
mag´ nāt

n. An important, often wealthy, person prominent in a large industry or business.
Andrew Carnegie was the steel **magnate** who endowed 2,800 libraries across the country.

misnomer
mis nō´ mər

n. A name that does not fit.
"Vegetable" is sometimes considered to be a **misnomer** for the tomato, since tomatoes are actually classified as fruits.

onerous
än´ ər əs

adj. Burdensome; oppressive.
After working hard all day, my mother considers cleaning up after us an **onerous** task.

pandemonium
pan də mō´ nē əm

n. A state or place of great confusion or uproar.
A shout of "Fire!" created **pandemonium** in the crowded theater.

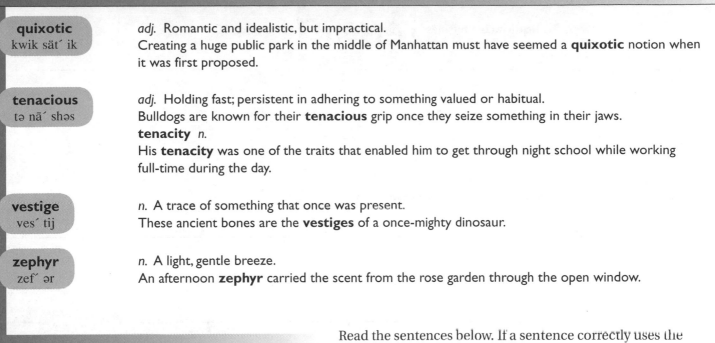

quixotic kwik sät´ ik	*adj.* Romantic and idealistic, but impractical. Creating a huge public park in the middle of Manhattan must have seemed a **quixotic** notion when it was first proposed.
tenacious tə nā´ shəs	*adj.* Holding fast; persistent in adhering to something valued or habitual. Bulldogs are known for their **tenacious** grip once they seize something in their jaws. **tenacity** *n.* His **tenacity** was one of the traits that enabled him to get through night school while working full-time during the day.
vestige ves´ tij	*n.* A trace of something that once was present. These ancient bones are the **vestiges** of a once-mighty dinosaur.
zephyr zef´ ər	*n.* A light, gentle breeze. An afternoon **zephyr** carried the scent from the rose garden through the open window.

9A Understanding Meanings

Read the sentences below. If a sentence correctly uses the word in bold, write *C* on the line below it. If a sentence is incorrect, rewrite it so that the vocabulary word in bold is used correctly.

1. A **constraint** is something that is unchanging.

2. An **onerous** task is one that is difficult.

3. Something that is **gossamer** is light enough to float in the air.

4. A **vestige** is a small trace that remains.

5. **Tenacity** is a firmness of purpose.

6. A **flotilla** is a gentle breeze.

7. To **liquidate** a business is to sell its property to raise cash.

8. A **cautionary** message is one that points out possible dangers.

9. A **zephyr** is a hot-air balloon.

10. A **misnomer** is a nickname.

11. An **ignominious** departure is one made hurriedly.

12. **Pandemonium** is a place of great excitement.

13. A **magnate** is a person of great wealth and influence.

14. To **incur** something is to relieve oneself of it.

15. A **quixotic** plan is one that may have little chance of success.

cautionary
constrain
flotilla
gossamer
ignominious
incur
liquidate
magnate
misnomer
onerous
pandemonium
quixotic
tenacious
vestige
zephyr

9B Using Words

If the word (or a form of the word) in bold fits in a sentence in the group below it, write the word in the blank. If the word does not fit, leave the space empty.

1. **tenacious**

   (a) He was given a _____ gift for his graduation.

   (b) There was little the Dolphins could do to break the Jaguars' _____ hold on their lead.

   (c) We need something a little more _____ than this flimsy tape.

2. **onerous**

   (a) The pay is good and the hours are short, but the work is _____ .

   (b) The _____ task of deciding the defendant's fate falls upon the jury.

   (c) She had the _____ responsibility of having to pay all the bills.

3. **vestige**

   (a) A man garbed in the _____ of a monk opened the door and let us enter.

   (b) Terry's bearded _____ was captured for all time by his brother's camera.

   (c) Of the meadows where I played as a child not a _____ remained.

4. **constrain**

   (a) She was too independent to let everyday conventions _____ her actions.

   (b) Each branch of government acts as a _____ on the other two.

   (c) We had to _____ the unruly dog.

5. **liquidate**

   (a) Ice begins to _____ when the temperature rises above 32°F.

   (b) I should be able to get $10,000 if I _____ all my stock holdings.

   (c) The crime boss did not hesitate to _____ anyone who stood in his way.

6. **cautionary**

   (a) It would be wise to use a _____ until she finds out more about the situation.

   (b) "The Boy Who Cried Wolf" is a _____ tale about how misfortunes can result from lying.

   (c) My advice was intended to be _____ , and you weren't obligated to heed it.

7. **incur**

   (a) Keep a record of the costs you _____ in carrying out the project.

   (b) You will _____ the teacher's wrath if you continue to disrupt the class.

   (c) The stray dog seemed more like an _____ than a family pet.

8. **ignominious**

(a) The life of pirate Rachel Wall came to an _____ end on the gallows.

(b) I had to admit I was quite _____ of the cause of the car's engine failure.

(c) He was such an _____ that he lost his keys every week.

9C Word Study

Choose from the two words provided and use each word only once when filling in the spaces. One space should be left blank.

quixotic/impractical

1. It is _____ to try to tickle oneself.

2. Rearranging the seating at this late date would be _____.

3. The president's plan for people to live on Mars by the year 2004 seemed _____ to many.

condone/excuse

4. If you are finished, you may _____ yourself from the table.

5. If we do not challenge offensive behavior, others may think we _____ it.

6. He knelt before his angry wife and asked her to _____ him.

chary/hesitant

7. "I . . . I'm not sure," was Spencer's _____ reply.

8. "I was _____ of the scheme from the start," said one investor crossly.

9. Since I feel _____, I made a decision right away.

exodus/departure

10. Fear of imminent flooding caused the sudden _____ from the valley.

11. The flight attendant announced a delay in the plane's _____.

12. The _____ of leaves in the fall is a sign of impending winter.

circuitous/indirect

13. The roller coaster follows a _____ route, including many twists and turns.

14. The shape is so _____, it's difficult to describe in words.

15. A small smile was his _____ way of showing approval of the plan.

cautionary
constrain
flotilla
gossamer
ignominious
incur
liquidate
magnate
misnomer
onerous
pandemonium
quixotic
tenacious
vestige
zephyr

9D Images of Words

Circle the letter of each sentence that suggests the numbered bold vocabulary word. In each group, you may circle more than one letter or none at all.

1. **flotilla**

   (a) The bride was accompanied by six bridesmaids and four flower girls.

   (b) Two dozen canoes approached the bank.

   (c) The president's motorcade was escorted by a swarm of motorcycle police.

2. **tenacity**

   (a) She held on to the side of the helicopter until it landed safely.

   (b) Jonah was uncertain whether to move across town.

   (c) Her persistence helped her to get the job.

3. **pandemonium**

   (a) There were eight dogs, all barking and rushing around at once.

   (b) There was a stunned silence when his aunt showed up unexpectedly.

   (c) The storm raged through the night but did little damage.

4. **cautionary**

   (a) Remembering Dad's lecture, I buckled my seatbelt.

   (b) Lauren's teacher gave her a stern look when he saw her passing notes.

   (c) They tested the X-17 rocket and found a few minor design flaws.

5. **quixotic**

   (a) I think Derrick should reconsider his plan to paddle alone across the Pacific in a canoe.

   (b) I never know when James is joking and when I should take him seriously.

   (c) Even though he has no experience with or knowledge of politics, he's planning to run in and win the next U.S. presidential election.

6. **gossamer**

   (a) A square yard of the tissue-like fabric weighs almost nothing.

   (b) "And the fairy's wings," said the storyteller, "were spun from cobwebs."

   (c) Hannah has lost so much weight that I hardly recognized her.

7. **zephyr**

   (a) The warm breeze barely ruffled the surface of the lake.

   (b) The stars shone brightly in the clear moonless sky.

   (c) He loved his lessons on the delicate stringed instrument.

8. **constraint**

   (a) I don't have enough time to tell you everything that happened.

   (b) Because money is short, we're only going for a very short vacation this year.

   (c) Trappist monks take a vow of silence.

9. **misnomer**

   (a) She was freed after posting bail.

   (b) Pleasant Street turned out to be a row of decrepit and abandoned houses.

   (c) Liberty Hall had so many rules that we were afraid to do anything.

10. **magnate**

    (a) Margaret Thatcher became Britain's first female prime minister in 1979.

    (b) The African lion is known as "the king of beasts."

    (c) Henry Ford's company became the largest maker of cars in the world.

9E Passage

Read the passage below; then complete the exercise that follows it.

Human-Powered Flight

An ancient Greek legend tells of Icarus, who, with wings made of feathers and wax, flew too close to the sun. The wax melted and Icarus fell to earth. This **cautionary** tale did not deter Paul MacCready, a pioneer in human-powered flight, who believed that humans, like birds, could fly with muscle power alone. His story began in 1959, when a British engineering **magnate** named Henry Kremer offered a cash prize for the first successful human-powered flight.

The rules of the offer stipulated that the craft had to complete a figure-eight course around two poles and clear a ten-foot-high obstacle at both the start and finish. The prize, worth 50,000 pounds (about $129,000 at the time), was still unclaimed in 1976, despite numerous attempts. In July of that year, a man named Paul MacCready began designing a craft that might capture the Kremer Prize. MacCready owned a boat-building company that had **incurred** debts totaling $90,000; he hoped to use the prize money to **liquidate** his company's debt. He must also have been motivated by the challenge, since entering such a difficult contest is a **quixotic** plan for earning money.

The pilot of MacCready's craft was a 135-pound, twenty-three-year-old amateur cyclist and hang glider pilot named Bryan Allen. As the power source for the human-powered aircraft, Allen would have the **onerous** task of pedaling with about four times the amount of force needed to pedal a bicycle. The chief **constraint** in designing the aircraft was to make it as light as possible while retaining strength and rigidity. So MacCready made the wings and cabin surfaces out of Mylar, a thin, light plastic. As a result, the aircraft had a **gossamer** lightness and fragility, which partially inspired its name, the *Gossamer Condor.** Even with a wingspan of ninety-six feet (longer than that of a DC-9 jet airplane), the total weight of the craft was kept to an incredible seventy pounds.

Before attempting to capture the Kremer Prize, Bryan Allen made many preliminary flights. Then, on August 23, 1977, at a small California airfield, he made the official attempt. By 7:30 a.m. the wind had become nothing more than a **zephyr**, and Allen was given the signal to begin pedaling. The first obstacle was cleared, with feet to spare. The big propeller, connected by a

cautionary
constrain
flotilla
gossamer
ignominious
incur
liquidate
magnate
misnomer
onerous
pandemonium
quixotic
tenacious
vestige
zephyr

*A condor is a very large vulture.

chain to Allen's pedals, turned so slowly its revolutions could easily be counted. The *Gossamer Condor* moved forward at a leisurely eleven miles per hour as the onlookers below watched with mounting excitement. The craft then passed easily over the finish-line obstacle and completed the 2,000-yard course in seven and a half minutes. **Pandemonium** broke loose among the spectators as the *Condor* gently landed. MacCready had won the Kremer Prize!

Two weeks later, Henry Kremer announced another prize. He would give 100,000 pounds (about $258,000) for the first successful human-powered flight across the twenty-two-mile-wide English Channel. So on June 12, 1979, Bryan Allen took off from the English coast in the successor to the *Condor*, the newly designed *Gossamer Albatross*.* Since a secondary meaning of albatross is "an obstacle to success," it might seem that MacCready was tempting fate. But it turned out that *Albatross* was a **misnomer** because all went well as the frail craft headed for Cap Gris-Nez, France.

Accompanied by a **flotilla** of fifteen small boats filled with spectators, Allen flew the *Albatross*. But after two and a half hours, and with the French coast in sight, it appeared that the last **vestige** of Allen's strength was leaving him, and he feared that the flight would end **ignominiously** in the sea just yards from the shore. Sheer **tenacity** kept him pedaling. Spectators in the boats and on shore cheered themselves hoarse as they saw the *Albatross* come floating above the beach and make a gentle turn. Then, after nearly three hours, Allen stopped pedaling, and the *Albatross* made a perfect landing on the sand.

* An albatross is a large seabird.

Answer each of the following questions in the form of a sentence. If a question does not contain a vocabulary word from this lesson's word list, use one in your answer. Use each word only once.

1. Was Kremer a successful businessperson?

2. What quality did MacCready need in order to succeed in his seemingly impractical quest?

3. Why was Mylar used to cover the aircraft's frame?

4. What **constraints** were placed on the path and height of the aircraft?

5. How would a **zephyr** help flying conditions?

6. Why did the name *Albatross* turn out to be a **misnomer**?

7. How was Allen **incurring** risk on his flight to France?

8. Why was Allen's task considered **onerous**?

9. Describe the scene on the beach when the *Albatross* landed.

10. How much of MacCready's debt did his total winnings allow him to **liquidate**?

FUN & FASCINATING FACTS

The Latin word *magnus* means "great" and forms the root of many English words. *Magnitude* (Lesson 8) is greatness of size or importance. *Magna* Carta is the great charter granting civil liberties to England, signed by King John in 1215. A *magnanimous* person is one who shows greatness of spirit. To *magnify* something is to make it seem greater than it really is. A *magnificent* display is one marked by the greatness of its splendor. And a **magnate** is a businessperson of great power and wealth.

The hero of Miguel de Cervantes' great comic romance, written in Spain in the early 1600s, is Don Quixote, "the knight of the woeful countenance," whose name is also the title of the book. Don Quixote is totally caught up in the romance of noble deeds, utterly idealistic without a shred of practicality in his makeup. This memorable character is the inspiration for the adjective associated with his name. A *quixotic* endeavor is a noble but unrealistic pursuit.

The ancient Greeks believed that a multitude of gods existed in nature. One of these was *Zephyrus*, god of the west wind, which was noted for its gentleness. The name survives in English as **zephyr**, a gentle breeze.

Lesson 10

Word List
Study the definitions of the words below; then do the exercises for the lesson.

attest
ə test´

v. To declare or be evidence of something as true, genuine, or accurate.
The constant long lines at Romolo's bakery **attest** to its popularity.

axiom
ak´ sē əm

n. A statement or principle that requires no proof because its truth is obvious.
My pleasure-loving aunt believes in the **axiom** that no one lives forever.
axiomatic *adj.*
The fact that no one can be in two places at once is **axiomatic**.

churlish
churl´ ish

adj. Lacking good manners; rude, impolite.
Barrett's **churlish** remarks started an altercation.

concoct
kən kakt

v. To make up, prepare, or invent.
We were able to **concoct** a delicious meal from the leftovers in the refrigerator.
concoction *n.*
The drink he created was a **concoction** of mango, pineapple, and grapefruit juice.

derivative
də riv´ ə tiv

n. Something that grows out of or results from an earlier form or condition.
The artificial sweetener saccharin is a **derivative** of coal tar.
adj. Based on what has gone before; lacking originality.
The artist's work is **derivative** of the Flemish school of painting.

differentiate
dif ər en´ shē āt

v. 1. To see the difference; to distinguish.
The twins looked so much alike I could not **differentiate** between them.
2. To be or make different.
Her expressive way of playing the piano **differentiated** her from the other contestants.

disparage
dis par´ ij

v. To criticize in a negative, disrespectful manner.
I didn't mean to **disparage** your relationship with Corey when I said that he was not a loyal person.
disparaging *adj.*
Her **disparaging** remarks about his artwork did not discourage him from applying to art school.

dissipate
dis´ i pāt

v. 1. To break up and spread out so thinly as to disappear; to scatter or be scattered.
The sun **dissipated** the morning fog.
2. To spend or use foolishly.
He **dissipated** his inheritance in six months and has now incurred heavy debts.

esoteric
es ə ter´ ik

adj. Not generally known or understood; familiar to only a relatively small number of people.
Arabic used to be so **esoteric** that almost no one in America studied it, but it has become much more popular recently.

olfactory
äl fak´ tər ē

adj. Relating to the sense of smell.
His **olfactory** sense told him that he was close to a chocolate factory.

plethora
pleth´ ə rə

n. Too great a number; an excess.
Of the **plethora** of suggestions, there were a few that were useful.

| **refurbish** rē fər´ bish | *v.* To make like new; to renovate. We **refurbished** the guest room before our cousins came to stay with us. |

secrete
sə krēt´

v. 1. To produce and give off.
Enzymes **secreted** by the stomach aid in digestion.
2. To place so as to be hidden from view; to conceal.
The money was **secreted** in a hidden compartment of the suitcase.

vagary
vā´ gər ē

n. (usually plural) A departure from the normal, expected course; a whim or unpredictable action.
The **vagaries** of the marketplace make it difficult to predict how well the stock market will perform each year.

volatile
väl´ ə təl

adj. 1. Evaporating quickly.
Gasoline is a **volatile** substance.
2. Changing readily; explosive; unpredictable.
Emotions run high when people discuss a **volatile** subject like abortion.

10A Understanding Meanings

Read the sentences below. If a sentence correctly uses the word in bold, write *C* on the line below it. If a sentence is incorrect, rewrite it so that the vocabulary word in bold is used correctly.

1. An **olfactory** organ is one that responds to sounds.

2. A **concoction** is something prepared by combining various ingredients.

3. To **disparage** a performance is to belittle it.

4. A **churlish** person is one who seeks to please others.

5. **Vagaries** are departures from what might be expected.

6. A **plethora** of vegetables is an oversupply of them.

attest
axiom
churlish
concoct
derivative
differentiate
disparage
dissipate
esoteric
olfactory
plethora
refurbish
secrete
vagary
volatile

7. To **differentiate** between plans is to note the differences in them.

8. To **attest** to a fact is to give evidence of it.

9. A **volatile** economy is one that changes rapidly.

10. To **refurbish** a product is to take it off the market.

11. An **esoteric** subject is one that is obscure.

12. An **axiom** is a statement that appears to contradict itself.

13. To **secrete** a substance is to produce and release it.

14. To **dissipate** a crowd is to work it up into a frenzy.

15. A **derivative** poem is one that is not innovative.

10B Using Words

If the word (or a form of the word) in bold fits in a sentence in the group below it, write the word in the blank. If the word does not fit, leave the space empty.

1. **differentiate**

   (a) Farley complained there was little to _____ Republicans from Democrats.

   (b) My views _____ from hers on a number of key points.

   (c) His smart appearance and alert bearing _____ him from his coworkers.

2. **derivative**

   (a) Their competition against each other in the race had a _____ effect on their friendship.

   (b) His so-called research is completely _____ and therefore inconsequential.

   (c) Orlon fiber is a _____ of natural gas, oxygen, and nitrogen.

3. **refurbish**

   (a) You could use this roll of green velvet to _____ that worn-out sofa.

   (b) Hailey is planning to buy that old house, _____ it, and then sell it at a profit.

   (c) Sid tends to _____ the truth about what happened to make a better story.

4. **plethora**

   (a) The _____ of attractions in Paris cannot be taken in on a single short visit.

   (b) The _____ of footnotes makes up a third of the book's total length.

   (c) Will returned from his "trick or treat" outing with a _____ of candy.

5. **attest**

   (a) There are several witnesses who can _____ to the man's innocence.

   (b) We can't accept these claims until we've had an opportunity to _____ them.

   (c) Having used that cleanser for some time, I can _____ to its effectiveness.

6. **volatile**

   (a) Welfare reform was a _____ political issue in the 1990s.

   (b) His _____ nature makes him unpredictable and difficult to deal with.

   (c) Water becomes _____ when heated to the boiling point.

7. **dissipate**

   (a) It took several hours for the smoke from the fire in the kitchen to _____ .

   (b) She condemned youths who _____ their energies in local pool halls.

   (c) The young man was able to _____ into the crowd, and we lost him.

attest
axiom
churlish
concoct
derivative
differentiate
disparage
dissipate
esoteric
olfactory
plethora
refurbish
secrete
vagary
volatile

8. concoct

    (a) The alibi they tried to _____ could not withstand the court's scrutiny.

    (b) Try this _____ of corn flakes, chocolate syrup, marshmallows, and walnuts.

    (c) After the radio failed, we lost all _____ with the airplane.

10C Word Study

Fill in the missing word in each of the sentences below. Then write a brief definition of the word. The number in parentheses shows the lesson in which the word appears.

1. The prefix *epi-* means "upon." It combines with the Greek *taphos* (a tomb) to form the English

    word _____ (7).

    Definition: _____

2. The Latin *tenax* means "holding fast." It forms the English word _____ (9).

    Definition: _____

3. The prefix *con-* means "together." It combines with the Latin *coqere* (to cook) to form the English

    word _____ (10).

    Definition: _____

4. The Latin *magnus* means "great." It forms the English word _____ (8).

    Definition: _____

5. The prefix *eu-* means "good" or "well." It combines with the Greek *phemos* (speech) to form the

    English word _____ (6).

    Definition: _____

6. The Latin *vagus* means "wandering." It forms the English word _____ (10).

    Definition: _____

7. The Latin *olere* (to smell) and *facere* (to make) combine to form the English word _____

    (10).

    Definition: _____

8. The Latin prefix *circum-* means "around." It combines with the Latin *venire* (to go) to form the

    English word _____ (6).

    Definition: _____

9. The Latin *melior* means "better." It forms the English word _____ (6).

Definition: _____

10. The Latin *volere* means "to fly." It forms the English word _____ (10).

Definition: _____

10D Images of Words

Circle the letter of each sentence that suggests the numbered bold vocabulary word. In each group, you may circle more than one letter or none at all.

1. **axiom**

   (a) A triangle has three angles.

   (b) Everyone had a mother at one time.

   (c) Increased specialization in industry leads to increased efficiency.

2. **differentiate**

   (a) He couldn't determine which ring had the genuine diamond and which had the fake one.

   (b) Paula assures us that this kind of mushroom isn't poisonous.

   (c) Stars remain fixed, while planets move across the night sky.

3. **esoteric**

   (a) The contract was written in legal language that was difficult for the average person to understand.

   (b) Tonight's topic is the evolution of Vedic into classical Sanskrit literature.

   (c) The chapter on the event horizon of black holes is especially fascinating.

4. **vagaries**

   (a) It's hard to keep up with current fashions since they change so often.

   (b) New England weather is notoriously unpredictable.

   (c) The mayor changes her mind so often that no one knows where she stands.

5. **volatile**

   (a) The meteorite struck the earth with enormous force.

   (b) The cologne will evaporate unless you keep the bottle tightly closed.

   (c) Tamara flies off the handle at the slightest provocation.

6. **churlish**

   (a) The wagon wheels were up to their axles in mud, making progress difficult.

   (b) You mean to say Rodney took the money and didn't even thank you for it?

   (c) The room needed fresh paint and some pictures on the walls.

attest
axiom
churlish
concoct
derivative
differentiate
disparage
dissipate
esoteric
olfactory
plethora
refurbish
secrete
vagary
volatile

7. **disparage**

(a) She beat the school record in the hundred-meter dash.

(b) These sandwiches taste like sawdust.

(c) Six minutes elapsed before the second-place runner crossed the finish line.

8. **secrete**

(a) The function of the tear ducts is to keep the surface of the eye moist.

(b) I didn't know the concrete was still wet until I stepped in it.

(c) The best hiding place for my wallet was under the mattress.

9. **dissipate**

(a) Since I last weighed myself, I have lost two pounds.

(b) When we got to Beacon's Cross, we decided to go our separate ways.

(c) The grocery bill at ValuShop came to thirty-two dollars.

10. **olfactory**

(a) One's hearing becomes less acute as one gets older.

(b) My new glasses give me 20/20 vision.

(c) The sense of smell is especially well developed in dogs.

10E Passage

Read the passage below; then complete the exercise that follows it.

The Sweet Smell of Success

With over 800 fragrances on the market and a new one appearing almost every week, the perfume business is very competitive. Creating a distinct, new fragrance is both complicated and expensive; each manufacturer seeks to **differentiate** its perfume from the **plethora** of others on the market. This process begins with the "nose," a person with a keen **olfactory** sense, who helps **concoct** new perfumes by combining up to several hundred ingredients from the thousands available. The manufacturer's goal is to produce a fragrance that the public will find irresistible.

To develop a new perfume, the "nose" tries to balance three key ingredients, called "notes." The top notes are the more **volatile**, easily accessible aromas such as lemon or orange. These provide the initial tang to a perfume and give potential buyers their first impression. Floral smells from jasmine, iris, or rose oil, a **derivative** of rose petals from Bulgaria, are often the source of the middle notes, also known as the "heart notes;" they give richness and body to the fragrance. The base notes come from ingredients such as sandalwood or cedar and provide what is called the "dry-down," the smell that lingers after the fragrance has dried on the skin.

Increasingly, synthetic ingredients are being used in creating perfumes. They are usually cheaper and can cut the cost of a fragrance by as much as three-quarters. Furthermore, they greatly extend the range of possibilities available to the "nose." They are also readily available and not subject to the uncertainties of the weather: the harvest of Bulgarian rose petals, for example, can be ruined by a hot, dry spell at the wrong time.

Synthetic substances have also replaced two ingredients that were once used to "fix" the various oils in perfume to ensure that the fragrance did not **dissipate** once the bottle was opened. They are ambergris, a grayish wax found in the intestines of sperm whales, and musk, the strong-smelling substance **secreted** by a gland in the stomach of the male musk deer. Because they were derived from endangered species, both products are now banned by international agreements.

Once a new perfume has been created by the "nose" and approved by the maker, attention turns to the name, the packaging, and the commercial launch of the perfume. While all three are important, no one factor can guarantee success, for there is a saying in the trade that "in the end, the perfume decides." In spite of the **vagaries** of the marketplace, however, once a perfume wins acceptance, it can create a strong consumer loyalty. The success of some perfumes is **attested** to by the fact that they remain best-sellers for generations.

Since the perfume business is a worldwide one, the name chosen is usually one that can be easily pronounced in many languages; a conscientious manufacturer considers thousands of possible names before making a decision. The final choice may be a word that is familiar, or it may be something more **esoteric**, perhaps a name taken from a language such as Sanskrit, that suggests mystery and romance.

The packaging consists of the bottle holding the perfume, the box it comes in, and the point-of-sale advertising material. The shape, size, color, and overall design of each package are carefully engineered to give the product both a timeless quality and a fashionable look. A design that is too trendy at the time it is introduced, but which quickly becomes dated and in need of **refurbishment** within a few years, would be a costly mistake.

The introduction of a new perfume is critical to its success and can cost tens of millions of dollars. It often begins with a trade party, perhaps held in an exotic location, to which hundreds of guests from the fashion business and media are invited, all expenses paid. The manufacturer hopes that none of the recipients of such largesse would be so **churlish** as to **disparage** the product after being so lavishly entertained. After all, it is **axiomatic** that most people do not bite the hand that feeds them.

Who pays for all this? Ultimately, the consumer does. An expensive perfume might sell for as much as $150 an ounce. The total cost of that bottle's contents? Anywhere from $5 to $10.

Answer each of the following questions in the form of a sentence. If a question does not contain a vocabulary word from this lesson's word list, use one in your answer. Use each word only once.

1. What quality must a perfume blender have?

| attest |
| axiom |
| churlish |
| concoct |
| derivative |
| differentiate |
| disparage |
| dissipate |
| esoteric |
| olfactory |
| plethora |
| refurbish |
| secrete |
| vagary |
| volatile |

2. What does the "nose" do?

3. What are top notes?

4. What is rose oil?

5. What is musk?

6. What advantages do perfume makers gain from using synthetic ingredients instead of plant **derivatives**?

7. What were ambergris and musk used for?

8. How might a perfume maker attempt to **refurbish** a poorly selling product?

9. Why might a perfume manufacturer give a perfume an **esoteric** name?

10. Why do perfume makers entertain guests from the fashion and media industries so lavishly?

FUN & FASCINATING FACTS

In England, a thousand years ago, a member of the poorest or peasant class was called a *ceorl*. Over the centuries, the word changed to *churl* and acquired a negative meaning. It eventually dropped out of use, although the adjective form **churlish** has survived.

When George Washington became ill in 1799, his condition was diagnosed as **plethora**, an excess of blood in the body. Doctors treated this condition by bleeding the patient. No one was ever cured by this treatment, which contributed to the deaths of many patients, including Washington. The practice was eventually abandoned, but the word survives, referring to a general oversupply. The word is formed from the Latin word *plere*, "to fill." Other words sharing this root include *complete*, *replenish*, and *deplete*.

Lesson 11

Word List

Study the definitions of the words below; then do the exercises for the lesson.

agrarian
ə grer´ ē ən

adj. Having to do with farming or agriculture.
At the state fair, everyone was talking about the grain harvest and other **agrarian** concerns.

burgeon
bər´ jən

v. To grow and expand rapidly; to flourish.
The **burgeoning** population of Las Vegas puts a strain on the area's resources.

cataclysm
kat´ ə kliz əm

n. A sudden and violent change; a catastrophe.
It would take a long time to rebuild the city of New Orleans fully after the **cataclysm** of 2005's Hurricane Katrina.
cataclysmic *adj.*
The area survived several **cataclysmic** events, including a tornado and a flood.

culinary
kyoo´ li ner ē

adj. Having to do with cooking.
Julia Child, a well-known cookbook author and chef, had a great deal of **culinary** expertise.

denigrate
den´ i grāt

v. To attack the reputation of; to criticize in a derogatory manner.
The sales manager **denigrated** his competitors' products.

gourmet
goor mā´

n. A person who likes fine food and is a good judge of its quality.
To his great satisfaction, the meal Tom had spent hours preparing was fit for a **gourmet**.
adj. She is willing to spend the extra money to go to **gourmet** restaurants because she loves good food.

grandiloquent
gran dil´ ə kwənt

adj. Using lofty or pompous speech or expression.
He began in **grandiloquent** fashion by addressing his listeners as "My fellow toilers in the vineyard of scientific truth."
grandiloquence *n.*
The **grandiloquence** of her writing was meant to impress her teacher.

hybrid
hī´ brid

n. 1. The offspring of two animals or plants of different species or varieties.
The sweet corn **hybrid** is disease resistant.
2. Anything that is of mixed origin or composition.
The committee is a **hybrid**; it consists of people from all of the performing arts.
adj. Creole is a **hybrid** language composed of French, Spanish, and African dialects.

manifold
man´ ə fōld

adj. Having many different kinds, forms, or parts.
As head of the student council, her duties were **manifold**: she did everything from stuffing envelopes to addressing the PTA.

palatable
pal´ ət ə bəl

adj. Acceptable or pleasing, especially to the sense of taste.
Although raw fish didn't sound very appetizing to me, it was, in fact, surprisingly **palatable**.

panacea
pan ə sē´ ə

n. Something that is supposed to cure all ills or difficulties; a cure-all.
Nuclear power plants were once hailed as the **panacea** for the world's energy problems.

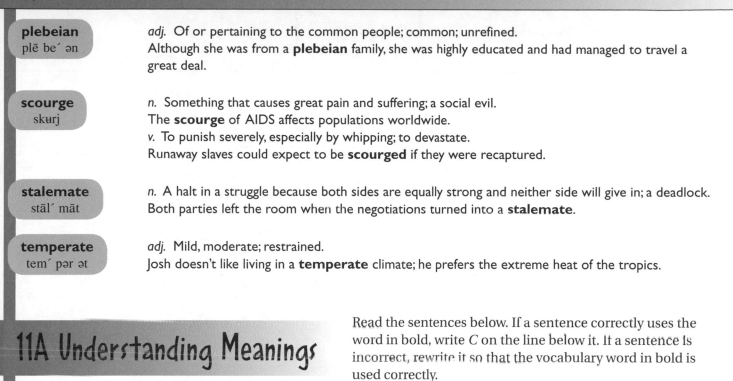

plebeian
plē be´ ən

adj. Of or pertaining to the common people; common; unrefined.
Although she was from a **plebeian** family, she was highly educated and had managed to travel a great deal.

scourge
skʉrj

n. Something that causes great pain and suffering; a social evil.
The **scourge** of AIDS affects populations worldwide.
v. To punish severely, especially by whipping; to devastate.
Runaway slaves could expect to be **scourged** if they were recaptured.

stalemate
stāl´ māt

n. A halt in a struggle because both sides are equally strong and neither side will give in; a deadlock.
Both parties left the room when the negotiations turned into a **stalemate**.

temperate
tem´ pər ət

adj. Mild, moderate; restrained.
Josh doesn't like living in a **temperate** climate; he prefers the extreme heat of the tropics.

11A Understanding Meanings

Read the sentences below. If a sentence correctly uses the word in bold, write *C* on the line below it. If a sentence is incorrect, rewrite it so that the vocabulary word in bold is used correctly.

1. **Temperate** behavior is marked by self-control and patience.

_____

2. A **cataclysm** is a sudden change for the better.

_____

3. To **scourge** someone is to inflict severe punishment on that person.

_____

4. **Grandiloquence** is the use of pompous language.

_____

5. A **stalemate** is an advantage that one side holds in a confrontation.

_____

6. **Agrarian** concerns are those relating to agriculture.

_____

7. A **hybrid** community is one composed of people of various backgrounds.

8. To **denigrate** something is to ridicule it.

9. To be **plebeian** is to be commonplace and unpolished.

10. A **burgeoning** community is one that has great difficulties.

11. **Culinary** tools are those used in agriculture.

12. A **gourmet** is a person who enjoys good food, expertly prepared.

13. A **panacea** is a specific solution for one problem.

14. A person who has **manifold** duties has numerous tasks to juggle.

15. A **palatable** dish is one that tastes good.

agrarian
burgeon
cataclysm
culinary
denigrate
gourmet
grandiloquent
hybrid
manifold
palatable
panacea
plebeian
scourge
stalemate
temperate

11B Using Words

If the word (or a form of the word) in bold fits in a sentence in the group below it, write the word in the blank. If the word does not fit, leave the space empty.

1. **culinary**

   (a) The new TV series on the _____ arts features a number of famous chefs.

   (b) Among the common _____ herbs are mint, marjoram, basil, and rosemary.

   (c) My _____ skills are limited, but I can make a first-class omelet.

2. **panacea**

   (a) Penicillin was once considered a _____ for infectious diseases.

   (b) Honey and lemon is an excellent _____ for a sore throat.

   (c) Beware of politicians who promise a _____ for all the country's ills.

3. **scourge**

   (a) The hurricane _____ the countryside.

   (b) The spread of nuclear weapons is a _____ that threatens the human race.

   (c) Search vessels _____ the ocean floor hoping to locate the sunken ship.

4. **gourmet**

   (a) The dish was served in a small china _____ decorated with vine leaves.

   (b) The main course was a _____ dish of shrimp and scallops served over rice.

   (c) I'm no _____ , but I know a good Maryland crabcake when I taste one.

5. **cataclysm**

   (a) A full-scale nuclear war would be the most _____ event in history.

   (b) We suffered a _____ when one of the wheels came off the toy buggy.

   (c) Global warming could raise sea levels and trigger a worldwide _____ .

6. **hybrid**

   (a) Montreal has a _____ culture of French- and English-speaking inhabitants.

   (b) The liger is a _____ that has a lion and a tiger as its parents.

   (c) I am a _____ whenever I go to a strange city.

7. **manifold**

   (a) The _____ uses of the peanut make it a popular agricultural commodity.

   (b) He performed his _____ duties promptly and efficiently.

   (c) Buffalo were once _____ but are now greatly reduced in number.

8. **plebeian**

(a) He dropped his _____ ways and assumed the identity of an aristocrat.

(b) His _____ tastes tend toward hot dogs and pizza rather than caviar and truffles.

(c) Lincoln's _____ origins did not deter him from seeking the United States presidency.

11C Word Study

Each group of four words below contains two words that are either synonyms or antonyms. Circle these two words; then circle the *S* if they are synonyms, the *A* if they are antonyms.

1. servile	colloquial	inexorable	subservient	S	A
2. interment	rendition	procedure	burial	S	A
3. largesse	gesture	stipend	salary	S	A
4. laceration	decline	translation	resurgence	S	A
5. colloquial	vital	inconsequential	tenacious	S	A
6. reminiscent	idealistic	circuitous	direct	S	A
7. trace	flotilla	vestige	routine	S	A
8. cautionary	dignified	delicate	ignominious	S	A
9. calm	volatile	axiomatic	shapeless	S	A
10. depend	deny	attest	refurbish	S	A

agrarian
burgeon
cataclysm
culinary
denigrate
gourmet
grandiloquent
hybrid
manifold
palatable
panacea
plebeian
scourge
stalemate
temperate

11D Images of Words

Circle the letter of each sentence that suggests the numbered bold vocabulary word. In each group, you may circle more than one letter or none at all.

1. **grandiloquence**

(a) Every mother's son and every father's daughter will be there.

(b) He wore a green velvet coat, satin breeches, and a tall hat with a feather.

(c) In the summertime, the garden was a mass of flowers of every color.

2. **cataclysm**

(a) The Mariana Trench near Guam is the deepest known part of the Pacific Ocean.

(b) In 1890, between 200 and 400 Sioux men, women, and children were massacred by U.S. government troops during a conflict known as the Battle of Wounded Knee.

(c) The eruption of the Krakatoa volcano in 1883 was one of the most violent in history.

3. **hybrid**

   (a) This vehicle, which is part car and part boat, can travel on the road and on water.

   (b) Ann Ross and Sam Brinkley changed their last names to Brinkley-Ross when they got married.

   (c) Mules are half horse and half donkey.

4. **burgeon**

   (a) Thanks to Johnny Appleseed, orchards sprang up throughout the Ohio Valley.

   (b) The number of community theaters grew rapidly in the 1960s.

   (c) We discovered that a water pipe had burst and flooded the cellar.

5. **agrarian**

   (a) Throughout the 1800s, the greater part of the population grew their own fruits and vegetables.

   (b) Ant farms are popular with people who like insects.

   (c) Plowing, planting, and harvesting marked the passage of the seasons.

6. **scourge**

   (a) The Great Plague of London killed about 75,000 people from 1664 to 1666.

   (b) She cried when she skinned her knee.

   (c) After the dinner party, Nate had a lot of pots and pans to clean.

7. **temperate**

   (a) The island has a comfortable, year-round temperature between 70°F and 75°F.

   (b) He is always diplomatic, even when we strongly disagree.

   (c) There was little to set Elisa's house apart from the others on the street.

8. **stalemate**

   (a) Neither country could back down from the growing crisis.

   (b) The two athletes were considered equally good tennis players.

   (c) Talks resumed for the ninth time today with no agreement in sight.

9. **palatable**

   (a) Mondrian used a narrow range of colors in his geometric paintings.

   (b) The soup was so bland and flavorless that I couldn't finish it.

   (c) The water that came from the spring was fresh and pleasant-tasting.

10. **denigrate**

   (a) You're wasting your time working here, for the job has no future.

   (b) Looking grave, the doctor told Sean that he was very sick.

   (c) The old car began to rust and needed more and more repairs every year.

11E Passage

Read the passage below; then complete the exercise that follows it.

Boiled, Baked, Mashed, or French Fried?

Potatoes rank with rice and wheat as one of the world's main food crops. They are highly **palatable** and nutritious, providing vitamin C, protein, thiamine, and amino acids. In addition to being served alone, potatoes are also ground into flour that can be used in baking, and as a thickener in sauces and soups. Recently this **plebeian** vegetable has become fashionable in **culinary** circles. Many supermarkets now offer a wider range of potatoes because of their popularity. Snowflake, Black Russian, Pink Pearl, and Mrs. Moherle's Yellow are just a few of the more than 200 varieties currently available. **Gourmets** have even enjoyed seven-course all-potato dinners prepared by great chefs, beginning with potato soup and ending with potato-and-black-truffle ice cream!

The importance of the potato dates back centuries. Indigenous to South America, the potato was first cultivated there by **agrarian** societies as early as 1,800 years ago. The potato was introduced to Europe in the 1500s, where it was initially viewed with grave suspicion. Those who **denigrated** the potato falsely accused it of being poisonous and the cause of the prevalent diseases of the time.

Eventually, however, Europeans came to appreciate the potato's **manifold** virtues. They learned that it had many advantages over the grains they relied on at the time. Potatoes could be stored easily over the winter, and they were not as subject to spoilage due to insects or disease. In addition, one acre of potatoes produced four times as much food as an acre of wheat or rye.

In 1777, Austria went to war with its neighbor, Bavaria, over who could become the next Bavarian monarch. There was relatively little fighting during this war because the two countries spent most of their energy stealing potatoes and other supplies from one another. Ultimately, Austria and Bavaria ran out of potatoes and the conflict settled into a **stalemate**. This event was popularly known as the Potato War, although its **grandiloquent** title is the War of Bavarian Succession.

A tragic event related to the potato was the Irish Potato Famine, in the mid-nineteenth century. The British government controlled Ireland and forced the Irish to maintain relatively small farms. As a result, the cultivation of the potato **burgeoned** in Ireland because it yields a relatively large amount of food in a small amount of space. By the mid-nineteenth century, the people of Ireland had become economically dependent on this crop. The typical Irish peasant family of the period sustained itself almost exclusively on a diet of potatoes. Then, in 1845, a disaster of **cataclysmic** proportions struck. Blight, a plant disease affecting the leaves and roots, destroyed the entire Irish potato crop. Over a million people died of starvation and related diseases because of the British policies on Ireland, which treated the poor harshly and played a role in bringing about needless deaths. To escape the **scourge**, an equal or greater number of Irish emigrated to other countries, mostly to the United States.

In Peru, the birthplace of the potato, scientists at the International Potato Center at Molina, work to preserve the vegetable's full genetic diversity and to create new **hybrid** forms that are disease resistant and can thrive even in tropical as well as **temperate** climates. Although it is a **panacea** for world hunger, the potato plays a significant role in fulfilling the world's nutritional needs.

agrarian

burgeon

cataclysm

culinary

denigrate

gourmet

grandiloquent

hybrid

manifold

palatable

panacea

plebeian

scourge

stalemate

temperate

Answer each of the following questions in the form of a sentence. If a question does not contain a vocabulary word from this lesson's word list, use one in your answer. Use each word only once.

1. Why is the potato referred to as a **plebeian** vegetable?

2. Who would be more likely to be interested in "designer" potatoes?

3. What **culinary** feats have some chefs performed with the potato?

4. Who first cultivated the potato?

5. Why did Europeans develop a **burgeoning** interest in the potato?

6. What **scourge** struck Ireland in 1845?

7. Why is the War of Bavarian Succession a **grandiloquent** title?

8. How did the Potato War end?

9. Why are tropical climates less suitable for growing potatoes?

10. What are scientists at the International Potato Center at Molina working on?

FUN & FASCINATING FACTS

Gourmet and *gourmand* are similar in meaning, but there is a slight difference that should be noted. A *gourmet* is a lover of food who takes great interest in its preparation and consumption. A *gourmand* has similar tastes but the word suggests that such a person favors quantity over quality.

The Greek word *pan* means "all." It is combined with the Greek *akos*, "a cure," to form **panacea**, a cure-all.

In ancient Rome, the members of the ruling class were called patricians. The name was derived from the Latin word *pater*, "father." The rest of the population was made up of the common people, or **plebeians**, from the Latin *plebius*, "of the common people." The *plebeians* waged a long struggle to obtain political equality with the patricians and had succeeded in their efforts by around 300 B.C. *Plebeian* survives as an adjective in modern English.

Lesson 12

Word List

Study the definitions of the words below; then do the exercises for the lesson.

aftermath
af´ tər math

n. A consequence or result, often a negative one.
Thousands of people were left without shelter in the **aftermath** of the earthquake.

aphorism
af´ ər iz əm

n. A short statement of truth or principle; an adage.
My mother often warned me to slow down, citing the **aphorism**, "Haste makes waste."

catharsis
kə thär´ səs

n. A releasing of the emotions, often through the arts, that brings about spiritual renewal or a relieving of tension.
By drawing pictures reflecting their traumatic experiences, children often experience **catharsis**.
cathartic *adj.*
Rina found talking to the guidance counselor a **cathartic** experience.

cohort
kō´ hôrt

n. 1, A group that is moving or working together.
The president was followed by a **cohort** of media people.
2. One who assists another, especially in a dubious or criminal activity; an accomplice.
He denied being a **cohort** of the crime boss.

culpable
kul´ pə bəl

adj. Deserving blame or censure.
Because of his negligence, the driver of the car that crashed was found **culpable**.
culpability *n.*
Her **culpability** was publicized in the newspapers, but she persistently maintained her innocence.

diabolical
dī ə bäl´ i kəl

adj. Devilish; wicked or evil.
The **diabolical** plot to assassinate the chief justice was discovered before it could be implemented.

enormity
ē nôr´ mə tē

n. 1. The state or quality of being monstrous or outrageous.
After the dictator was toppled from power, the **enormity** of his crimes was revealed.
2. The state or quality of being huge, immense.
Some people are skeptical of Japan's plan to erect a mile-high skyscraper because of the **enormity** of the project.

gibe
jīb

v. To utter taunting, sarcastic words.
The fans **gibed** at the referee for ignoring the deliberate foul.
n. A taunting, scornful remark.
Andrew's **gibe** about Liza's new glasses really hurt her feelings.

innocuous
i näk´ yōō əs

adj. Harmless; unlikely to offend.
The reporter's question seemed **innocuous**, yet I was chary of giving out any information.

necessitate
nə ses´ ə tāt

v. To require; to make necessary.
This new situation **necessitates** a different approach to the problem.

odyssey
äd´ ə sē

n. 1. A long, adventurous journey.
My South American **odyssey** took me through half a dozen countries and lasted almost six months.
2. An intellectual or spiritual quest.
His political **odyssey** took him from socialism in his youth to arch-conservatism in old age.

partisan
pärt´ i zən

n. 1. A strong supporter or advocate.
The young volunteers were **partisans** of the newest candidate for mayor.
2. An armed fighter opposed to an occupying army.
Marshal Tito's band of **partisans** harassed the German army that occupied Yugoslavia.
adj. Strongly biased in favor of a particular party, cause, or position.
Because of her **partisan** politics, Tina votes Republican in every election.

posterity
päs ter´ ə tē

n. A person's descendants; future generations.
Is it quixotic to want to make the world a better place for **posterity**?

premeditated
prē med´ ə tāt əd

adj. Fully planned beforehand; deliberate.
The lawyer argued that the defendant's action was impulsive and not **premeditated**.

scurrilous
skʉr´ ə ləs

adj. Vulgar; coarsely abusive.
These **scurrilous** rumors were perpetrated by someone trying to denigrate your character.

12A Understanding Meanings

Read the sentences below. If a sentence correctly uses the word in bold, write *C* on the line below it. If a sentence is incorrect, rewrite it so that the vocabulary word in bold is used correctly.

1. A **premeditated** act is one carried out by someone under the influence of medication.

2. To **necessitate** change is to require it or make it necessary.

3. A **diabolical** scheme is one that is absurdly complicated.

aftermath
aphorism
catharsis
cohort
culpable
diabolical
enormity
gibe
innocuous
necessitate
odyssey
partisan
posterity
premeditated
scurrilous

4. A **catharsis** is a spiritual or mental renewal.

5. A **partisan** is someone who is ambivalent.

6. An **odyssey** is anything that is strange or out of the ordinary.

7. The **enormity** of the task was overwhelming.

8. An **innocuous** remark is one that expresses rancor.

9. **Posterity** refers to the generations who come after.

10. An **aphorism** is a grandiloquent way of saying something.

11. **Scurrilous** language is abusive and indecent.

12. To be **culpable** is to be liable or blameworthy.

13. A **cohort** is a person's companion or supporter.

14. A **gibe** is an attempt to cheat someone.

15. The **aftermath** of an event is the result that follows.

12B Using Words

If the word (or a form of the word) in bold fits in a sentence in the group below it, write the word in the blank. If the word does not fit, leave the space empty.

1. **scurrilous**

   (a) A mouse made its _____ way across the floor and quickly disappeared.

   (b) These _____ attacks on the mayor's wife are a low point in the campaign.

   (c) Their remarks, though _____, did not intimidate me in the slightest.

2. **cohort**

(a) The government official used to ride in a _____ during parades.

(b) I agree with his views, but to call me a _____ of the senator is absurd.

(c) The doctor made his rounds accompanied by a _____ of medical students.

3. **enormity**

(a) The _____ of the homework assignment caused the students to groan.

(b) Robert McNamara admitted the _____ of his error in escalating the Vietnam War.

(c) The car's speed is _____ .

4. **partisan**

(a) A _____ captured by the occupying army could expect no mercy.

(b) She writes frankly as a _____ of the extreme left wing of the party.

(c) The board is a _____ body and can't be expected to give impartial rulings.

5. **culpable**

(a) If you encouraged them to commit the crime, then you are also _____ .

(b) Regarding the break-in, the gatekeeper was _____ , at least to the extent that she failed to check the locks.

(c) Even though he could not have prevented the accident, he still feels _____ .

6. **necessitate**

(a) The merger of our two chief competitors will _____ a change of our business strategy.

(b) Taking on extra staff would help to _____ the completion of the project.

(c) The flooding in the town will _____ taking a circuitous route to Albany.

7. **posterity**

(a) Among his _____ was a great-grandfather who served in Lincoln's cabinet.

(b) Let us preserve our national forests, not just for ourselves today, but for _____ .

(c) Some critics believe that this artist is ahead of his time and will be more appreciated by _____ .

8. **innocuous**

(a) Even an _____ greeting like "Hello" can sound sinister when said by a great character actor.

(b) She's so irritating and loud, she borders on being _____ .

(c) Because nobody respected his opinion, his criticisms were considered to be fairly _____ .

aftermath
aphorism
catharsis
cohort
culpable
diabolical
enormity
gibe
innocuous
necessitate
odyssey
partisan
posterity
premeditated
scurrilous

12C Word Study

Complete the analogies by selecting the pair of words whose relationship most resembles the relationship of the pair in capital letters. Circle the letter in front of the pair you choose.

1. ANCESTRY : POSTERITY ::
   (a) mother : father
   (b) church : state
   (c) grandfather : grandson
   (d) family : generation

2. RUDE : SCURRILOUS ::
   (a) illegal : legal
   (b) innocent : innocuous
   (c) brief : ephemeral
   (d) embarrassing : ignominious

3. OLFACTORY : NOSE ::
   (a) visual : eye
   (b) manual : hold
   (c) tasty : tongue
   (d) loud : ear

4. MAGNATE : BUSINESS ::
   (a) athlete : sports
   (b) president : country
   (c) name : misnomer
   (d) student : education

5. SHIP : FLOTILLA ::
   (a) journey : voyage
   (b) wing : bird
   (c) sail : rudder
   (d) bird : flock

6. SHOVEL : IMPLEMENT ::
   (a) stipend : largesse
   (b) toaster : appliance
   (c) bat : baseball
   (d) glove : mitt

7. CEDE : RETAIN ::
   (a) chase : follow
   (b) grip : grasp
   (c) require : necessitate
   (d) lose : gain

8. DESULTORY : METHODICAL ::
   (a) placid : rambunctious
   (b) dissatisfied : disgruntled
   (c) turbulent : tumultuous
   (d) responsible : culpable

9. GOSSAMER : COBWEB ::
   (a) insect : spider
   (b) coarse : rope
   (c) zephyr : breeze
   (d) calm : pandemonium

10. ABUNDANCE : PLETHORA ::
    (a) cause : aftermath
    (b) size : enormity
    (c) food : gourmet
    (d) cure-all : panacea

12D Images of Words

Circle the letter of each sentence that suggests the numbered bold vocabulary word. In each group, you may circle more than one letter or none at all.

1. **aphorism**

   (a) To a man with a hammer, everything looks like a nail.

   (b) If you should get lost, don't be afraid to ask for directions.

   (c) The darkest hour is just before the dawn.

2. **culpable**

   (a) He accidentally left the lantern in the barn, and the hay near it caught fire.

   (b) The soil in the region is so rich that it produces two or three crops a year.

   (c) Kyla always thinks she's right and refuses to give up in an argument.

3. **innocuous**

   (a) The children are due to receive their flu shots today.

   (b) The jury surprised everyone in the courtroom with its "not guilty" verdict.

   (c) She didn't do anything suspicious or wrong.

4. **aftermath**

   (a) We finished painting the room and took a break.

   (b) Widespread fires broke out following the 1906 San Francisco earthquake.

   (c) The breakup of Soviet Communism led to unrest throughout Russia.

5. **cohort**

   (a) The accused had no fewer than twelve lawyers defending him.

   (b) The Majority Leader could count on the loyal support of forty senators.

   (c) Lena is looking for a responsible person to accompany her to Egypt.

6. **catharsis**

   (a) The play's powerful climax had a deep, almost spiritual effect on the audience.

   (b) She had to wear the cast on her arm for six weeks.

   (c) Just being able to talk about the experience provided him with enormous relief.

7. **partisan**

   (a) Julian joined a group that was attempting to overthrow the dictator.

   (b) The speaker made his stand clear on the issue of gay rights.

   (c) I called Marla greedy because she took the last piece of cake.

aftermath
aphorism
catharsis
cohort
culpable
diabolical
enormity
gibe
innocuous
necessitate
odyssey
partisan
posterity
premeditated
scurrilous

8. **gibe**

   (a) The player with the ball swerved to avoid the linebacker rushing at him.

   (b) Everyone giggled when Mike called that skinny kid "Muscles."

   (c) José gave me a poke in the ribs that left a bruise.

9. **premeditated**

   (a) The prosecuting lawyer must prove that the accused intended to commit the crime.

   (b) We planned our trip from Seattle to Anchorage, Alaska, over a year ago.

   (c) A crime that took such careful planning was no spur-of-the-moment act.

10. **odyssey**

    (a) It took nine months for him to sail around the Mediterranean coastline.

    (b) Reading Trollope's novels is like traveling through mid-Victorian England.

    (c) The Voyager probes launched in 1977 are now far beyond our solar system.

12E Passage

Read the passage below; then complete the exercise that follows it.

A Witness

The Italian writer Primo Levi spent his entire life, except for a three-year absence **necessitated** by World War II, in the same house in Turin, Italy, where he was born in 1919. In 1943, Levi, a young chemistry graduate, left home to become a **partisan** in the struggle to free Italy from German occupation. Betrayed by an informer, Levi, who was Jewish, was arrested and sent to Auschwitz, the Nazi death camp in Poland.

There he experienced some of the horrors of the Holocaust, the **premeditated** mass murder of the Jews that Hitler and his **cohorts** organized. At the Holocaust's peak, the four huge gas chambers at Auschwitz killed 6,000 people a day. During his trial after the war, the commandant of the camp, Rudolf Hoess, admitted his **culpability** in countless murders. His **diabolical** acts included supervising the execution of two and a half million people; he was also responsible for the deaths of another half million, who starved.

Miraculously, Levi was still alive, though barely, when Auschwitz was liberated by Russian troops in early 1945, a few months before the war's end. Later that year, after a six-month **odyssey** by train that took him deep into Russia, he was able to return to his home in Turin. There he picked up the threads of his life and outwardly led a normal and comfortable existence. He married, raised a family, and pursued a career as a chemical engineer. But the **enormity** of the crimes he had witnessed weighed heavily on him. Beginning in 1947, with *Survival in Auschwitz*, Levi wrote a series of books that dealt with his wartime experience and its **aftermath**.

Primo Levi was one of only three of the 650 Italian Jews crammed into a train bound for Auschwitz who lived. Writing was a **catharsis** for him, a way of coming to terms with his feelings of guilt for having survived when so many had died. In one of his essays, he suggests that the reason to write is "to free oneself from anguish." But his overriding concern was to ensure that **posterity** would have a clear picture of what had happened. He was haunted by the **gibes** that Nazis made at him, claiming that the world would never find out the truth, "[for] none of you will be left to bear witness . . . And even if some proof should remain and some of you survive, people will say that the events you describe are too monstrous to be believed."

In fact, as early as 1947, books denying that the Holocaust occurred began to appear in a number of countries. In the United States, the **innocuous**-sounding Institute for Historical Review was founded in 1978. Its purpose was to promote the **scurrilous** view that the Holocaust was a hoax, the gas chambers never existed, and the deaths in the camps were caused by starvation due to Allied bombing that disrupted supplies.

By placing full-page advertisements in college newspapers calling for a "full and fair debate" and calling on readers to consider "both sides" of the issue, the so-called institute hoped to sow doubts in the minds of students.

🔊   These efforts to distort and obscure what happened bear out the **aphorism** that "uncomfortable truths travel with difficulty." Levi knew people would find it hard to believe that events so unimaginable actually happened. In his writings, he tried to ensure that the truth as he knew it was exposed for the whole world to see.

Answer each of the following questions in the form of a sentence. If a question does not contain a vocabulary word from this lesson's word list, use one in your answer. Use each word only once.

1. Why did Levi initially leave home?

2. What did Levi witness at Auschwitz?

3. Did Rudolf Hoess try to defend himself at his trial?

4. What did Levi do after his release from Auschwitz?

5. What is his book *Survival in Auschwitz* about?

6. How was writing about the Holocaust emotionally helpful for Levi?

7. What motivated Levi to write about his wartime experiences?

8. Why was Levi worried that future generations might not find out about the truth of the Holocaust?

aftermath
aphorism
catharsis
cohort
culpable
diabolical
enormity
gibe
innocuous
necessitate
odyssey 🔊
partisan
posterity
premeditated
scurrilous

9. Why does the passage say that the name Institute for Historical Review is not as **innocuous** as it sounds?

10. What **aphorism** does Levi quote about our resistance to accepting unpleasant truths?

FUN & FASCINATING FACTS

A **cohort** used to refer to one of the ten divisions of a Roman legion of between 300 and 600 men. With the collapse of the Roman Empire, *cohort* came to mean any large group. More recently, *cohort* also refers to a companion or associate, usually with a negative connotation. One is more likely to read of a gangster's *cohorts* than, for instance, a government official's *cohorts*.

Gibe, meaning "to taunt," may also be spelled *jibe*. *Gibe* has just this one meaning, but *jibe*, in addition to being the alternative spelling of *gibe*, has two other meanings: "to change course suddenly while sailing" and "to be in agreement with."

The **Odyssey** is the title of a long epic poem, written some time before 700 B.C. and credited to the ancient Greek poet Homer. The poem tells of the ten-year wanderings of Odysseus, a Greek leader of the Trojan War. An **odyssey** is any extended journey of adventure or discovery, either literal (Columbus's *odyssey* resulted in Europeans' settling in the Americas) or metaphorical (Freud's *odyssey* into the mysteries of the human mind can be traced in his collected works).

Review for Lessons 9-12

Crossword Puzzle Solve the crossword puzzle below by studying the clues and filling in the answer boxes. Clues followed by a number are definitions of words in Lessons 9 through 12, except for 8 down, which is from an earlier lesson. The number gives the word list in which the answer to the clue appears.

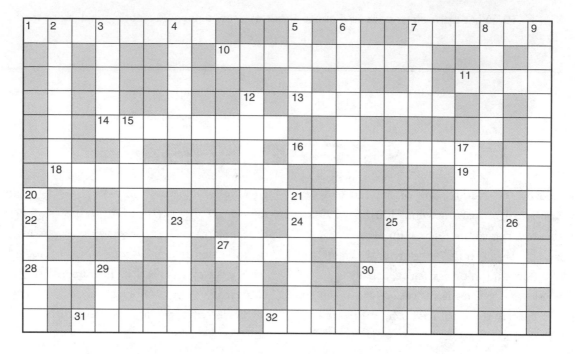

Clues Across

1. Evaporating quickly (10)

7. To declare something as true (10)

10. Harmless; unlikely to offend (12)

11. "The Garden of _____"

13. A wealthy and important businessperson (9)

14. A name that does not fit (9)

16. A group of ships (9)

18. Vulgar; coarsely abusive (12)

19. Opposite of *future*

22. Not generally known or understood (10)

24. Opposite of *lose*

25. One who assists in a dubious activity (12)

27. A taunting remark (12)

28. A trumpet, for example

30. A strong supporter or advocate (12)

31. Something that causes great suffering (11)

32. A trace of something that once was present (9)

Clues Down

2. Troublesome or burdensome (9)

3. A statement whose truth is obvious (10)

4. Students should _____ in school.

5. "Ode to a Nightingale," for example

6. Developing and growing; flourishing (11)

7. Abbreviation for "assistant"

8. To provide with a gift

9. Firmness in holding on (9)

12. To make like new (10)

15. Jewish state

17. A short statement of truth or principle (12)

20. A light, gentle breeze (9)

21. A dozen

23. To bring upon oneself, as a debt (9)

26. Mark _____, famous American author

29. Abbreviation for most populated American city

Lesson 13

Word List
Study the definitions of the words below; then do the exercises for the lesson.

adjunct
a´ juŋkt

n. Something or someone joined or added to something else but not essentially a part of it.
The roadside stand was an **adjunct** to the orchard's pick-your-own apples business.

belie
bē lī´

v. To give a false impression of; to contradict.
His temperate tone **belied** the inflammatory content of his speech.

carnage
kär´ nij

n. Great destruction of life; slaughter.
An entire generation recoiled in horror from the **carnage** of World War I.

dilemma
di lem´ ə

n. A problem that seems to have no satisfactory solution; a difficult choice.
His **dilemma** was whether to go to his daughter's play or his son's recital, both of which were on the same night.

diverse
də vurs´

adj. Differing from one another; having various or distinct parts.
The fair had a **diverse** selection of food; everything from Italian and French to Ethiopian and Indian cuisine was available.
diversity *n.*
When I hear the various languages people speak on the streets of my neighborhood, I am struck by its **diversity**.

eradicate
ē rad´ i kāt

v. To get rid of; to uproot.
The goal of the literacy project is to **eradicate** illiteracy.

flout
flout

v. To ignore in a disrespectful or scornful way.
Miranda **flouted** convention by wearing jeans to graduation.

foment
fō ment´

v. To stir up, to rouse; to instigate.
In the 1960s, anti-war activists **fomented** student demonstrations and strikes that shook the Johnson and Nixon administrations.

insurrection
in sər ek´ shən

n. An open revolt against legal authority; a rebellion.
According to Lincoln, the Confederacy's withdrawal from the Union was an **insurrection**.

mandatory
man´ də tôr ē

adj. Ordered by an authority; required.
Courses in English, math, and science are **mandatory** for all first-year students.

mitigate
mit´ ə gāt

v. To make or become less serious or severe; to ameliorate.
The unusually warm weather **mitigated** the effects of the ice storm by melting all the ice and snow.

pretext
prē´ tekst

n. An effort to conceal the real intention or state of affairs; an excuse.
He always went to that restaurant because he was infatuated with the waitress, but he made a **pretext** of going because of the food.

singular
siṅ´ gyə lər

adj. 1. Denoting a single person or thing, contrasted to more than one.
The pronoun "I" is **singular**; "we" is plural.
2. Extraordinary; exceptional.
Audiences were captivated by the **singular** beauty of Hermann Prey's voice.
3. Strange or unusual.
Sherlock Holmes referred to the bizarre circumstance as his most **singular** case.

somnolent
säm´ nə lənt

adj. 1. Tending to cause sleepiness.
The motion of the train had a **somnolent** effect, and I had to shake myself to stay alert.
2. Drowsy.
After many hours on duty, going on rounds made the young doctor even more **somnolent**.

stalwart
stôl´ wərt

adj. 1. Strong; sturdy.
The football squad was as **stalwart** a group as I'd seen in a long time.
2. Firm; resolute.
The American Civil Liberties Union is a **stalwart** defender of the Bill of Rights.

13A Understanding Meanings

Read the sentences below. If a sentence correctly uses the word in bold, write *C* on the line below it. If a sentence is incorrect, rewrite it so that the vocabulary word in bold is used correctly.

1. A **singular** event is one that is unique or different.

2. A **stalwart** person is one who can be trusted.

3. To **eradicate** a disease is to cure the patient of it.

adjunct
belie
carnage
dilemma
diverse
eradicate
flout
foment
insurrection
mandatory
mitigate
pretext
singular
somnolent
stalwart

4. A **mandatory** sentence is one that must be imposed by law.

5. An **insurrection** is a revolt against a legal authority.

6. A **dilemma** is a problem with no obvious satisfactory solution.

7. To **belie** a report is to give it one's full support.

8. An **adjunct** is something that occupies a nonessential position.

9. To **mitigate** conditions is to improve them.

10. A **pretext** is an excuse offered in order to conceal the truth.

11. A **somnolent** village is one that has an unpleasant atmosphere.

12. To **flout** a custom is to proselytize in favor of it.

13. **Carnage** is killing on a vast scale.

14. A **diverse** program is one with many different parts.

15. To **foment** a riot is to encourage it.

13B Using Words

If the word (or a form of the word) in bold fits in a sentence in the group below it, write the word in the blank. If the word does not fit, leave the space empty.

1. **mitigate**

   (a) The fact that he acted out of ignorance does not _____ the seriousness of the offense.

   (b) This new drug is supposed to _____ the symptoms of the disease.

   (c) The judge decided to _____ his sentence from a short prison term to a period of community service.

2. **diverse**

   (a) We will _____ traffic around Everett Avenue while road repairs are in progress.

   (b) The committee was a _____ group made up of volunteers from all over the world.

   (c) The magazine employs writers with _____ points of view.

3. **belie**

   (a) Her failure to return my calls _____ her promise that she would stay in touch.

   (b) Her pleasant voice and sweet smile _____ her sometimes violent temper.

   (c) The flag _____ in the breeze.

4. **flout**

   (a) The executives at the company believed they could _____ environmental laws with impunity.

   (b) He waved and _____ to spectators at the parade.

   (c) In the future, students who _____ the school's dress code will be disciplined.

5. **singular**

   (a) Professor Moriarty's sudden disappearance was a most _____ occurrence.

   (b) You are a _____ individual, unlike any other human being.

   (c) Their home was a place of _____ peace and serenity.

6. **somnolent**

   (a) The dog lying in the town square was _____ in the heat of the noonday sun.

   (b) _____ passengers on the bus stirred occasionally and went back to sleep.

   (c) The lecturer's droning voice had a _____ effect on the audience.

7. **foment**

   (a) The fiery speeches at the rally were clearly intended to _____ a rebellion.

   (b) The campus was in a _____ over the firing of a popular professor.

   (c) The broadcast failed to _____ an uprising as the radio announcer had intended.

adjunct
belie
carnage
dilemma
diverse
eradicate
flout
foment
insurrection
mandatory
mitigate
pretext
singular
somnolent
stalwart

8. **eradicate**

(a) The 1960s "Great Society" program aimed to _____ poverty in the United States.

(b) Ultrasound is used to _____ painful kidney stones without surgery.

(c) This spray will _____ dandelions without harming the lawn.

13C Word Study

Write the word from the pair above it that makes the most sense in each of the sentences. Use each word only once. If neither word fits, leave the space blank.

harmless/innocuous

1. The dog looks fierce, but he is actually _____ .

2. The fence was _____ against keeping out deer.

3. Although unpleasant, a cold is a(n) _____ illness because it doesn't have lasting effects.

ignore/flout

4. If you bring your own snacks into the movies, you deliberately _____ the rules.

5. Do not _____ your teacher's warning that you will be late for class.

6. He tried to _____ me by calling me "slow poke."

problem/dilemma

7. The _____ with your idea is it is much too complicated.

8. The birds were busy with the _____ of so many seeds scattered on the lawn.

9. My twin sisters faced the _____ of whether to attend the same college or be separated for the first time.

deliberate/premeditated

10. The arrow followed a _____ path before embedding itself in the tree.

11. If a crime is _____ , the penalty is likely to be more severe.

12. Refusing to shake hands was a _____ insult.

prepare/concoct

13. The tofu chili is very easy to _____ .

14. I do not believe the ridiculous stories you _____ !

15. The kit is easy to assemble and takes just ten minutes to _____ .

13D Images of Words

Circle the letter of each sentence that suggests the numbered bold vocabulary word. In each group, you may circle more than one letter or none at all.

1. **carnage**

   (a) Almost 40,000 soldiers were killed or wounded at the Battle of Gettysburg.

   (b) Heart disease is the leading cause of death among American adults.

   (c) The earthquake caused considerable property damage but few deaths.

2. **flout**

   (a) Joe instigated the food fight but managed to shift the blame onto others.

   (b) She always breaks the speed limit when she drives.

   (c) We knew Sam cheated at card games, but we could never catch him at it.

3. **stalwart**

   (a) The defenders at the Alamo refused to surrender despite overwhelming odds.

   (b) My friends stood by me and never wavered in their defense of my actions.

   (c) The boulder was too heavy for us to move without help.

4. **singular**

   (a) The earth is the only planet that we know of that is presently capable of supporting life.

   (b) We were struck by the unparalleled beauty of Saturn's rings.

   (c) Everything in my room was intact, just as I had left it.

5. **adjunct**

   (a) The course in CPR was outside the school's regular curriculum.

   (b) Fruit and vegetables are a vitally important part of one's diet.

   (c) They had a backup baby-sitter, in case their regular baby-sitter was unavailable.

adjunct

belie

carnage

dilemma

diverse

eradicate

flout

foment

insurrection

mandatory

mitigate

pretext

singular

somnolent

stalwart

6. **dilemma**

   (a) They had a hard time deciding whether to abandon their home or remain and put their lives at risk.

   (b) She had to decide whether to lower her business's prices to attract more customers, or attempt to make money by selling fewer products at a higher price.

   (c) This time Margot chose peach ice cream over butter pecan.

7. **mandatory**

   (a) You cannot get into that law school without a 3.0 grade point average.

   (b) Be sure to wipe your feet before you enter the building.

   (c) Parents should not deny their children a good education.

8. **insurrection**

   (a) Tamika flatly declared she was too old to have to go to bed at eight o'clock.

   (b) When Martin Luther rejected the teachings of Catholicism in 1517, beginning the Protestant Reformation, he was excommunicated.

   (c) At the beginning of the nineteenth century, the slaves of Haiti rose up against French rule and took over the island.

9. **pretext**

   (a) A stranger offered to take our picture and then ran off with my camera.

   (b) He had to read several chapters in order to prepare for the exam.

   (c) The fine print on the document was hard to read because it was so small.

10. **mitigate**

   (a) The rain washed away the pollen, which made my allergy symptoms disappear.

   (b) Lithium is known to prevent dramatic mood swings in manic-depressive patients.

   (c) My teacher agreed to raise my grade from a C+ to a B.

13E Passage

Read the passage below; then complete the exercise that follows it.

Leading the Way

Today, the immaculate lawns and weathered brick buildings of Berea College, set on 140 acres in eastern Kentucky, have the **somnolent** air of a quiet academic community. Its present state, however, **belies** its lively history, for Berea has been in the vanguard of the battle to **eradicate** social inequality in America for over 150 years.

The Reverend John Fee, a **stalwart** opponent of slavery, established Berea in 1855 as a one-room schoolhouse. The school **flouted** local customs by accepting both black and white students. To educate blacks in a slave state was a **singular** act of courage that challenged the defenders of slavery, who believed that Fee was **fomenting** rebellion among the slave population.

In 1859, rumors of a slave **insurrection** swept through eastern Kentucky. The rumors were unfounded, but provided John Fee's opponents with a **pretext** for closing the school and forcing its thirty-four students and teachers to leave Kentucky. Two years later the Civil War erupted. When the **carnage** ended in 1865, slavery was abolished and Fee returned to Kentucky to continue his life's work.

During his years in exile, Fee spent his time raising money, using it to transform Berea into an institution of higher learning. It was coeducational, the first racially integrated college in the South, and it actively recruited the children of newly freed slaves and impoverished whites from Appalachia. Tuition, books, and room and board were free to those unable to pay. Among its many distinguished graduates are Mary Britton, class of 1874, the first black woman doctor in Lexington, and Carter G. Woodson, class of 1903, a son of slave parents who today is acknowledged as "the father of black history."

In 1904, the college was faced with a difficult **dilemma**. The Kentucky legislature passed a law forbidding racially integrated schools. Berea had to choose between being an all-white or an all-black college. Because the number of white students outnumbered black students, the college's administrators decided to make Berea an all-white school. However, they tried to **mitigate** this outcome by establishing the Lincoln Institute, a black vocational school near Louisville.

In 1950, the Kentucky law was repealed, and black students were admitted to Berea once again. Today's Berea students come from **diverse** backgrounds, representing over fifty countries. Admission is highly competitive, since the college can accept only one out of every forty applicants.

Berea's tuition is still free, not only to those who need financial assistance, but to all students. In return for free tuition, a ten-to-fifteen hour per week work schedule is **mandatory** for all students. Students choose from over 140 different jobs. For example, the students sell crafts at annual sales that make over $2 million a year for the college. In addition, students staff the college's fifty-seven-room hotel.

In 1987, Berea established the New Opportunity School for Women as an **adjunct** to the college. It reaches out to women in the area, many of them trapped in seemingly hopeless and often abusive situations. The three-week program helps women smooth the transition to furthering their education or entering the job market. The program was started by Jane Stephenson, the wife of Berea's president, and is the latest chapter in a long and honorable tradition of working to provide equal opportunities in education.

Answer each of the following questions in the form of a sentence. If a question does not contain a vocabulary word from this lesson's word list, use one in your answer. Use each word only once.

1. What event in U.S. history resulted in enormous loss of life?

2. Why could Fee's opponents accuse him of **fomenting** conflict?

3. How does the author of the passage indicate that Fee was resolute in his opposition to slavery?

4. Why was Fee's school closed in 1859?

5. How did Berea change after 1904?

6. What effect did the 1904 Kentucky act have on education in the state?

7. How does Berea College **mitigate** its onerous financial burden?

adjunct
belie
carnage
dilemma
diverse
eradicate
flout
foment
insurrection
mandatory
mitigate
pretext
singular
somnolent
stalwart

8. Is the New Opportunity School for Women part of Berea?

9. What **dilemma** does the college admissions department face each year?

10. Why would it be inaccurate to describe the school's atmosphere in 1859 as **somnolent**?

FUN & FASCINATING FACTS

To **eradicate** weeds in the garden, one must pull them up by the roots. *Eradicate* is formed from the Latin *radix*, which means "root." Other words formed from this Latin word include *radish*, a root vegetable, and *radical*. A radical solution is one that goes to the root of the problem. *Radical* also refers to the root of a number, as in $3\sqrt{8} = 2$ (the cube root of 8 is equal to 2).

Sometimes the word **flout** is confused with the word *flaunt*. *Flout* means "to oppose openly and scornfully," whereas *flaunt* means simply "to display openly."

The Latin *somnus* means "sleep" and forms the root of several English words. People who have trouble sleeping are said to suffer from *insomnia*. The act of walking in one's sleep is called *somnambulism*. A person in a sleeplike state is said to be **somnolent**.

Lesson 14

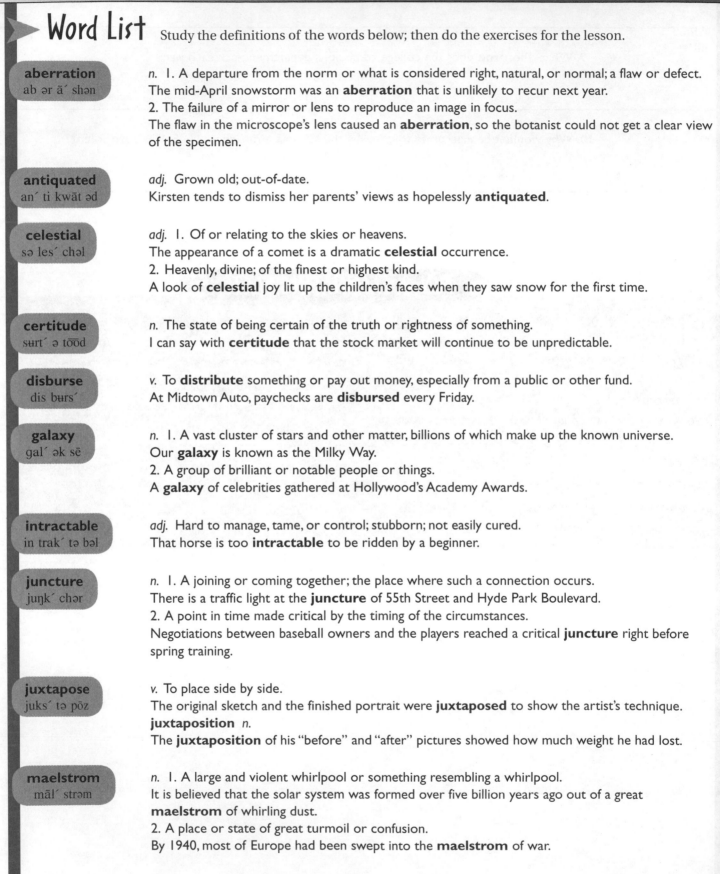

Word List Study the definitions of the words below; then do the exercises for the lesson.

aberration
ab ər ā´ shən

n. 1. A departure from the norm or what is considered right, natural, or normal; a flaw or defect.
The mid-April snowstorm was an **aberration** that is unlikely to recur next year.
2. The failure of a mirror or lens to reproduce an image in focus.
The flaw in the microscope's lens caused an **aberration**, so the botanist could not get a clear view of the specimen.

antiquated
an´ ti kwāt əd

adj. Grown old; out-of-date.
Kirsten tends to dismiss her parents' views as hopelessly **antiquated**.

celestial
sə les´ chəl

adj. 1. Of or relating to the skies or heavens.
The appearance of a comet is a dramatic **celestial** occurrence.
2. Heavenly, divine; of the finest or highest kind.
A look of **celestial** joy lit up the children's faces when they saw snow for the first time.

certitude
surt´ ə tōod

n. The state of being certain of the truth or rightness of something.
I can say with **certitude** that the stock market will continue to be unpredictable.

disburse
dis burs´

v. To **distribute** something or pay out money, especially from a public or other fund.
At Midtown Auto, paychecks are **disbursed** every Friday.

galaxy
gal´ ək sē

n. 1. A vast cluster of stars and other matter, billions of which make up the known universe.
Our **galaxy** is known as the Milky Way.
2. A group of brilliant or notable people or things.
A **galaxy** of celebrities gathered at Hollywood's Academy Awards.

intractable
in trak´ tə bəl

adj. Hard to manage, tame, or control; stubborn; not easily cured.
That horse is too **intractable** to be ridden by a beginner.

juncture
juŋk´ chər

n. 1. A joining or coming together; the place where such a connection occurs.
There is a traffic light at the **juncture** of 55th Street and Hyde Park Boulevard.
2. A point in time made critical by the timing of the circumstances.
Negotiations between baseball owners and the players reached a critical **juncture** right before spring training.

juxtapose
juks´ tə pōz

v. To place side by side.
The original sketch and the finished portrait were **juxtaposed** to show the artist's technique.
juxtaposition *n.*
The **juxtaposition** of his "before" and "after" pictures showed how much weight he had lost.

maelstrom
māl´ strəm

n. 1. A large and violent whirlpool or something resembling a whirlpool.
It is believed that the solar system was formed over five billion years ago out of a great **maelstrom** of whirling dust.
2. A place or state of great turmoil or confusion.
By 1940, most of Europe had been swept into the **maelstrom** of war.

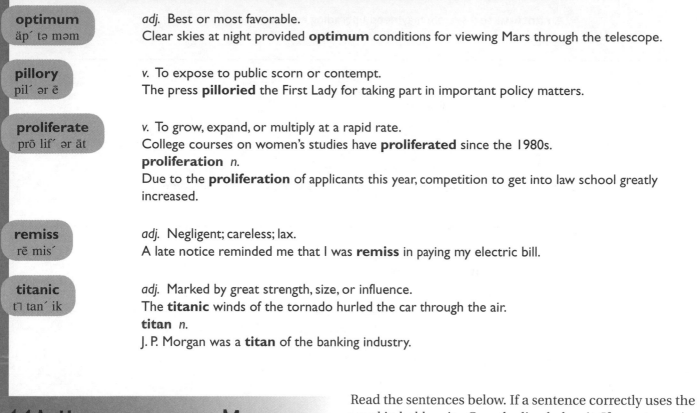

optimum
äp´ tə məm

adj. Best or most favorable.
Clear skies at night provided **optimum** conditions for viewing Mars through the telescope.

pillory
pil´ ər ē

v. To expose to public scorn or contempt.
The press **pilloried** the First Lady for taking part in important policy matters.

proliferate
prō lif´ ər āt

v. To grow, expand, or multiply at a rapid rate.
College courses on women's studies have **proliferated** since the 1980s.
proliferation *n.*
Due to the **proliferation** of applicants this year, competition to get into law school greatly increased.

remiss
rē mis´

adj. Negligent; careless; lax.
A late notice reminded me that I was **remiss** in paying my electric bill.

titanic
tī tan´ ik

adj. Marked by great strength, size, or influence.
The **titanic** winds of the tornado hurled the car through the air.
titan *n.*
J. P. Morgan was a **titan** of the banking industry.

14A Understanding Meanings

Read the sentences below. If a sentence correctly uses the word in bold, write *C* on the line below it. If a sentence is incorrect, rewrite it so that the vocabulary word in bold is used correctly.

1. A **titanic** effort is one that is desultory or ineffective.

2. A **galaxy** is a group of illustrious people.

3. **Celestial** music is music that seems to come from heaven.

4. A **maelstrom** is a whirlpool.

5. To **juxtapose** two objects is to place them next to each other.

6. An **antiquated** system may need upgrading or repairs.

7. A **juncture** is a turning point.

8. An **optimum** solution is one that offers the most favorable outcome.

9. An **aberration** is a departure from what is usual.

10. To **proliferate** is to scatter.

11. To be **remiss** is to fail to perform a duty.

12. **Certitude** is a false sense of security.

13. An **intractable** situation is one that is difficult to control.

14. To **pillory** someone is to make disparaging remarks to others about that person.

15. To **disburse** money is to hoard it.

aberration
antiquated
celestial
certitude
disburse
galaxy
intractable
juncture
juxtapose
maelstrom
optimum
pillory
proliferate
remiss
titanic

14B Using Words

If the word (or a form of the word) in bold fits in a sentence in the group below it, write the word in the blank. If the word does not fit, leave the space empty.

1. **celestial**

   (a) She enjoyed a year of _____ happiness as she realized her dream of traveling around the world.

   (b) The diagrams illustrate the sun, moon, and other _____ bodies.

   (c) Ian's _____ planning made the party a success.

2. **galaxy**

   (a) The awards dinner brought out a _____ of the town's leading citizens.

   (b) The sun and the nine planets that surround it make up our _____ .

   (c) The Andromeda _____ is composed of billions of stars and is located two million light-years from the Milky Way.

3. **aberration**

   (a) Even a small _____ in the engine will affect its performance.

   (b) His shoplifting habit indicates an _____ of character.

   (c) Normally, my dog is very friendly; all this barking is a complete _____ .

4. **intractable**

   (a) _____ problems have prevented the project from moving forward.

   (b) The detective had a hard time solving the case because the clues were _____ .

   (c) The cart was _____ in the deep mud.

5. **disburse**

   (a) The college will _____ the scholarship money in six-month installments.

   (b) I don't like to _____ eight dollars for a movie ticket.

   (c) After the speech, the crowd began to _____ .

6. **proliferate**

   (a) Dandelions _____ on the lawn in spite of our efforts to eradicate them.

   (b) Rumors _____ about the scandal.

   (c) Rail lines _____ throughout the country during the late 1800s.

7. **juxtapose**

   (a) Let us _____ for the sake of argument that two wrongs do make a right.

   (b) If you _____ the two pictures, you will see that they are not quite identical.

   (c) An elderly man got on the train and _____ himself behind me.

8. **titanic**

(a) An earthquake is the result of _____ forces far below the earth's surface.

(b) The _____ television show has lost its popularity in recent years.

(c) The leading computer manufacturer is also a _____ force in the development of software.

14C Word Study

The prefix *dis-* can mean "apart," "to remove," "completely," and "to deprive." **Note:** The "s" sometimes changes to another letter to make the word easier to say.

Fill in the missing word in each of the sentences below. The number in parentheses shows the lesson in which the word appears. Decide if the word begins with the prefix *dis-* and write the meaning from above if it does. If you think the word does not begin with a prefix having one of these meanings, leave the space blank.

1. If you _____ (10) someone, you are questioning that person's reputation.

   _____

2. A(n) _____ (13) is a difficult choice.

   _____

3. To _____ (14) money is to move it from the giver to the receiver.

   _____

4. A(n) _____ (6) object is one that is very small.

   _____

5. To _____ (3) between two things is to focus on their differences.

   _____

6. To _____ (10) is to recognize traits that make things different.

   _____

7. A(n) _____ (13) array is one with various and distinct parts.

   _____

8. To _____ (10) is to spread out so as to completely disappear.

   _____

aberration

antiquated

celestial

certitude

disburse

galaxy

intractable

juncture

juxtapose

maelstrom

optimum

pillory

proliferate

remiss

titanic

9. To be _____ (2) is to be completely dissatisfied.

_____

10. A(n) _____ (12) act is one that is wicked or evil.

_____

14D Images of Words

Circle the letter of each sentence that suggests the numbered bold vocabulary word. In each group, you may circle more than one letter or none at all.

1. **certitude**

   (a) I can't remember how to get to her house.

   (b) They were confident of the mountain's measurements, give or take 1,000 feet.

   (c) She was positive that the money was on the table when she left.

2. **intractable**

   (a) The dog was sent to obedience school after several failed attempts to train her.

   (b) I find it quite impossible to follow his reasoning in this article.

   (c) Finding a cure for cancer will be a long, difficult, and costly process.

3. **antiquated**

   (a) The pump used to draw water was a hundred years old, but it still worked.

   (b) This beautiful table is 200 years old and sold recently for $25,000.

   (c) Some laws are no longer appropriate or relevant in today's society, but because no one has bothered to change them, they are still in effect.

4. **celestial**

   (a) When it is noon in Greenwich, England, it is 5:00 a.m. in New York City.

   (b) The Roman god Pluto was the ruler of the underworld.

   (c) Sirius, known as the Dog Star, is the brightest star in the night sky.

5. **maelstrom**

   (a) Confused thoughts whirled in her head, making it difficult for her to think.

   (b) The water swirled in a great circle, sucking everything under.

   (c) The railroad station was a blur of rushing figures.

6. **proliferation**

   (a) Every ten years, the United States population increases by about ten million.

   (b) Last year there was an epidemic of the flu.

   (c) He loves to spend money on the most trivial gadgets.

7. **remiss**

   (a) He hasn't turned in his homework in two weeks.

   (b) They told me that it was unfortunate that I didn't get to see her recital because her performance was really good.

   (c) She missed her doctor's appointment for the third time in a row, without calling.

8. **optimum**

   (a) Now is the best time to plant those tomatoes.

   (b) For maximum fuel efficiency you should drive between fifty and fifty-five miles per hour.

   (c) I believe firmly that things always turn out for the best.

9. **juncture**

   (a) We'd reached a point where we either had to agree or break off negotiations altogether.

   (b) He was impressed with her kindness and sensitivity.

   (c) Beardstown is located where the Sangamon and Illinois rivers join.

10. **pillory**

   (a) At the press conference, his colleagues declared that he was unfit to hold public office.

   (b) Jane kicked Joseph because she said he had pulled her hair.

   (c) During the meeting, she ranted about her workers' incompetence.

14E Passage

Read the passage below; then complete the exercise that follows it.

Eye in the Sky

aberration
antiquated
celestial
certitude
disburse
galaxy
intractable
juncture
juxtapose
maelstrom
optimum
pillory
proliferate
remiss
titanic

Ever since Galileo constructed the first telescope in 1609, and used it to find four moons orbiting Jupiter, astronomers have been discovering more and more **celestial** bodies through the use of increasingly powerful instruments. Moons around Saturn, Uranus, and Neptune; the composition of the sun; and other stars and other galaxies have all been detected through telescopes.

In 1977, the National Air and Space Administration (NASA) began work on the Hubble Space Telescope (HST), a telescope that far outperformed any other in existence. As the work proceeded, costs began to exceed the original estimates and problems **proliferated**. NASA, under pressure to complete the project quickly, began to cut corners. The HST was completed and placed into Earth's orbit by the crew of the space shuttle *Discovery* in 1990.

In general, the images transmitted by earthbound telescopes are blurred as a result of distortion caused by the atmosphere. Located 365 miles above Earth, the HST would have the advantage of recording images outside of the atmosphere. Even under **optimum** conditions, the best telescopes would seem **antiquated** compared to the HST, which would transmit much clearer and crisper images.

But soon after the HST was launched, astronomers realized that it was seriously flawed. In their haste to complete the project, NASA had been **remiss** in the manufacture of the telescope. It turned out that the primary mirror was the wrong shape; its edges were too flat by one-fiftieth of the thickness of a human hair. Because of this error, the images recorded by the HST were fuzzy and out of focus.

NASA was **pilloried** by the press as well as by members of Congress who were responsible for **disbursing** money to NASA. Barbara Mikulski, head of the Senate committee that funds NASA, called the HST a "techno-turkey." To make matters worse, NASA endured another failure when it was unable to launch its probe to Mars as scheduled. This was a critical **juncture** for the space program. It needed to improve its success rate or lose the funding it needed to secure its future.

The problem with the HST proved to be **intractable**, but not insurmountable. The astronauts assigned to fix the HST went through more thorough practice sessions than those required for a typical space mission; their preparation included twice as much underwater training and the first virtual reality simulation training. Finally, in 1993, NASA sent the crew of seven astronauts aboard the shuttle *Endeavour* to repair the **aberration** in the HST's optical system. Fortunately for NASA, the mission was a success. Within weeks after the repair mission, NASA astronomers realized that the HST's optical system was even better than originally planned. The HST could see objects ten billion light-years away (one light-year is equal to about ten trillion miles). The HST was so powerful and precise that it could detect the light from a firefly 8,500 miles away. Photographs of remarkable clarity were **juxtaposed** with fuzzy ones taken earlier of the same regions in space. Mikulski, encouraged by the improvements, declared, "The trouble with Hubble is over . . . NASA has the right stuff."

One of the HST's greatest contributions to the field of astronomy is that it can transmit clearer images of celestial bodies and phenomena from a greater distance than earthbound telescopes can. One of the first phenomena recorded by the HST was a black hole. By definition, black holes are invisible because they have tremendously strong gravitational forces that suck in everything near them, including light. But the HST helped scientists detect this black hole because the telescope recorded the powerful effects that the black hole was having on other celestial matter. When astronomers observed images of **galaxy** M87, they noted a **maelstrom** of gases whirling at 1.2 million miles per hour! They surmised that these gases were being pulled by the **titanic** gravitational forces of a black hole. Astronomers can now say with absolute **certitude** that there is a black hole at the center of M87 that has as much matter as three billion suns, but is no larger than our solar system.

Answer each of the following questions in the form of a sentence. If a question does not contain a vocabulary word from this lesson's word list, use one in your answer. Use each word only once.

1. What **celestial** bodies did Galileo's telescope discern?

2. Did the process of developing the HST proceed as expected?

3. Why is the HST superior to earthbound telescopes?

4. In what respect was NASA culpable for Hubble's initial failure?

5. How did Mikulski **pillory** NASA in 1990?

6. Why was Mikulski's opinion of NASA important?

7. Could the problem with the HST be solved?

8. Why was a crew of seven astronauts sent aboard the *Endeavour*?

9. What became obvious when the later photographs from Hubble were placed next to the earlier ones?

10. What keeps the **maelstrom** of gases from flying away from M87's center?

FUN & FASCINATING FACTS

The Milky Way is the white band of stars that stretches across the night sky. Another name for the Milky Way is "the Galaxy," from the Greek word *gala*, meaning "milk." In the 1920s, astronomer Edwin Hubble (after whom the Hubble Space Telescope is named) discovered that the Galaxy was not unique, and that there are, in fact, billions of galaxies scattered throughout the universe. Following this discovery, the capital *g* was dropped and **galaxy** now refers to a collection of stars. Then, by extension, *galaxy* came to mean any gathering of movie stars or otherwise glamorous or distinguished people.

To **pillory** someone is to expose that person to public ridicule. The term is derived from a punishment common in colonial America. An offender was placed in a wooden framework with holes for the head and hands called a *pillory*. Unable to move, the offender was then subjected to various indignities inflicted by the local citizenry. This form of punishment has long been discontinued, but the word remains.

The Titans, in Greek mythology, were giants who ruled in heaven until they were overthrown by the god Zeus. The word **titan** is now used to describe a person of great accomplishment.

Lesson 15

Word List

Study the definitions of the words below; then do the exercises for the lesson.

abominate
ə bäm´ ə nāt

v. To hate or loathe intensely.
Many who **abominated** slavery worked unremittingly for its cessation.
abominable *adj.* 1. Detestable, loathsome.
Because of his **abominable** behavior, he had few friends.
2. Disagreeable and unpleasant.
She held her nose so that she couldn't smell the **abominable** odor coming from the dump.

abridge
ə brij´

v. To shorten in duration or extent; to diminish.
The publishers plan to **abridge** the 900-page novel to a more-manageable 600 pages.
abridged *adj.*
The **abridged** edition of *To Kill a Mockingbird* is easier to read, but I like the original better.

animosity
an ə mäs´ ə tē

n. Intense ill will.
His **animosity** was clear from the baleful looks he gave them.

auspicious
ôs pish´ əs

adj. Favorable, promising.
The speaker felt he was off to an **auspicious** beginning when the audience laughed at his opening anecdote.

beleaguer
bē lē´ gər

v. 1. To besiege; to surround with an army.
The small group of rebels was **beleaguered** by the well-trained army.
2. To surround with troubles; to harass.
The actress was **beleaguered** by the freezing theatre, the small audience, and her costar's cold.

confidant
kän´ fi dant

n. (spelled **confidante** when female) A person to whom secrets are told.
Not even the governor's closest **confidants** knew whether or not he would run for reelection.

constituent
kan stich´ o͞o ənt

n. 1. One of the parts that make up a whole.
Oxygen and nitrogen are the main **constituents** of the air we breathe.
2. A voter represented by a particular official.
The mayor of Santa Cruz met with her **constituents** after her election to office.

iniquitous
i nik´ wə təs

adj. Unjust; wicked.
The **iniquitous** practice of making young children work long hours has been banned in some countries but is still in effect in others.

inure
in yo͞or´

v. To adjust to and accept unpleasant or undesirable conditions.
People living on Blakeslee Street soon became **inured** to the smells from the nearby paper mill.

inveigh
in vā´

v. (used with *against*) To complain or protest strongly.
The newspaper's education columnist **inveighed** against the school's decision to institute an additional testing program.

predecessor
pred´ ə ses ər

n. A person or thing that has held a position or office before another.
President Clinton's **predecessor** was George H. W. Bush.

sabotage
sab´ ə täzh

n. Acts that intentionally damage, hinder, or seek to discredit.
Hiding the notes for my final report wasn't a practical joke, it was **sabotage**.
v. To engage in intentionally damaging acts.
Members of the French underground regularly attempted to **sabotage** trains bound for Nazi concentration camps.

sadistic
sə dis´ tik

adj. Taking pleasure in causing pain.
Some **sadistic** person thought it amusing to tie tin cans to the cat's tail.

scathing
skā´ thiŋ

adj. Harshly critical.
The author was devastated by the **scathing** reviews of his book; his previous book had been a best-seller.

transpire
tran spīr´

v. 1. To become apparent; to come to light.
It **transpired** that the two senators knew about the planned invasion all along.
2. To happen or occur.
The meeting that Chuck and Lisa had planned never **transpired**.

15A Understanding Meanings

Read the sentences below. If a sentence correctly uses the word in bold, write *C* on the line below it. If a sentence is incorrect, rewrite it so that the vocabulary word in bold is used correctly.

1. A meeting that **transpires** is one that actually takes place.

2. An **auspicious** beginning is one that bodes well for the future.

3. A **predecessor** is a person whose death occurs prematurely.

4. **Sabotage** is the malicious disruption of a thing or an activity.

5. To **inveigh** against someone is to win that person over by flattery.

6. The **constituents** of something are the parts that comprise it.

abominate
abridge
animosity
auspicious
beleaguer
confidant
constituent
iniquitous
inure
inveigh
predecessor
sabotage
sadistic
scathing
transpire

7. A **scathing** report is one that strongly condemns.

8. To **abridge** an article is to check it carefully for mistakes.

9. A **confidant** is someone with an overinflated opinion of his abilities.

10. A **sadistic** act is one perpetrated in secrecy.

11. To become **inured** to something is to get used to it.

12. **Animosity** is bitter hostility.

13. An **iniquitous** decision is one that is made in haste.

14. To **abominate** someone is to dislike that person intensely.

15. A **beleaguered** army is one that is heavily armed.

15B Using Words

If the word (or a form of the word) in bold fits in a sentence in the group below it, write the word in the blank. If the word does not fit, leave the space empty.

1. **auspicious**

   (a) This $1,000 donation is an _____ start to the fund-raising drive.

   (b) Finding a lucky four-leaf clover was regarded as an _____ sign.

   (c) I was feeling _____ so I bought a raffle ticket at the museum's fair.

2. iniquitous

(a) Slavery is commonly viewed as an _____ practice in the United States.

(b) The medicine had an _____ taste, but the nurse said it would do me good.

(c) The roofers did such an _____ job that it will have to be done over again.

3. abominate

(a) He was punished for his _____ behavior.

(b) Mother Teresa _____ the suffering of poor people in Calcutta, India, and worked for decades to help them.

(c) Shade-loving plants, including certain mosses, _____ strong sunlight.

4. inveigh

(a) Parents _____ against the cuts in funding for the schools.

(b) The forces _____ against us were so great that defeat was almost certain.

(c) The professor _____ against the unscientific manner of the experiment.

5. confidant

(a) We are _____ that the car will make it to Miami without breaking down.

(b) He had no _____ with whom he could share his misgivings.

(c) Harry Hopkins was a trusted _____ of Franklin Roosevelt's.

6. transpire

(a) It was unclear exactly what _____ as a result of the meeting.

(b) It later _____ that they had known each other all along.

(c) In her imagination she was _____ to the magical island ruled by Prospero.

7. scathing

(a) Such _____ criticism had an unnerving effect on the actor.

(b) Having survived a _____ ordeal, he naturally wanted time to rest.

(c) Several upsetting and _____ comments were made about him.

8. predecessor

(a) As the nation's first president, George Washington had no _____ .

(b) This legal ruling creates a _____ for other similar cases.

(c) The horse and buggy was the _____ of the automobile.

abominate

abridge

animosity

auspicious

beleaguer

confidant

constituent

iniquitous

inure

inveigh

predecessor

sabotage

sadistic

scathing

transpire

15C Word Study

Each group of four words below contains two words that are either synonyms or antonyms. Circle these two words; then circle the *S* if they are synonyms, the *A* if they are antonyms.

1. flout	endow	mitigate	aggravate	S	A
2. rancor	sabotage	plethora	animosity	S	A
3. puny	somnolent	volatile	stalwart	S	A
4. foment	imbue	instigate	eradicate	S	A
5. aberration	antiquated	cessation	flaw	S	A
6. singular	remiss	intractable	scrupulous	S	A
7. iniquitous	onerous	assiduous	diabolical	S	A
8. inure	transpire	intercede	occur	S	A
9. successor	predecessor	confidant	examiner	S	A
10. scathing	ominous	auspicious	ephemeral	S	A

15D Images of Words

Circle the letter of each sentence that suggests the numbered bold vocabulary word. In each group, you may circle more than one letter or none at all.

1. **beleaguer**

   (a) Reporters crowded the celebrity's front lawn, eager for a statement from him.

   (b) The fort's defenders held off the attackers until reinforcements arrived.

   (c) After a terrible season, fans, critics, and players of the football team demanded that the owner find a new coach.

2. **inure**

   (a) Over time, the night guard got used to sleeping days and working nights.

   (b) I keep a ten-dollar bill tucked away so that I'm never without money.

   (c) Baseball umpires soon learn to ignore the criticism of the fans.

3. abridge

(a) She thinks she sees a way to bring the two parties together.

(b) The novel's 632 pages have been cut to fewer than 300 in this edition.

(c) The new law requires anyone under eighteen to be off the streets by 10:00 p.m., if unaccompanied by an adult.

4. sabotage

(a) Brian passed a note to Marcela during the teacher's lecture.

(b) Someone damaged the printing press by putting sand in the gears.

(c) The candidate lost the election because of her serious errors of judgment.

5. scathing

(a) She claimed that she had never seen such a terrible performance in her life.

(b) The temperature last night dropped to six degrees below zero.

(c) His slovenly work habits have a detrimental effect on other employees.

6. constituent

(a) The universe is made up of matter and energy.

(b) It's about a thousand-mile drive from Vancouver to San Francisco.

(c) Each person in his district gets a monthly report from Congressman Wray.

7. animosity

(a) He was in such a bitter mood that he honked his car horn every chance he got on his way home.

(b) Jamie absolutely refuses to put skim milk on his breakfast cereal.

(c) The mere mention of her name makes him angry and upset.

8. predecessor

(a) If your wife dies before you, all the money from the trust goes to you.

(b) Somebody cut in front of me and took the only parking spot on the street.

(c) The Z-02 computer has been replaced by the more advanced Z-03 model.

9. inveigh

(a) They need to consider all of the possibilities before making a decision.

(b) Her teacher said there was room for improvement in her classroom behavior.

(c) The newspaper columnists think Savini has only a slim chance of being reelected.

10. sadistic

(a) The little boy loved to sit in the car and pretend he was driving.

(b) It's terrible to torture helpless animals.

(c) Sadie ran home in tears because the other children were teasing and taunting her.

abominate
abridge
animosity
auspicious
beleaguer
confidant
constituent
iniquitous
inure
inveigh
predecessor
sabotage
sadistic
scathing
transpire

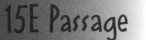

15E Passage

Read the passage below; then complete the exercise that follows it.

Mandela and the End
of Apartheid

When Nelson Mandela was sworn in in May of 1994 as South Africa's first black president, his **predecessor**, former president F. W. de Klerk, stood next to him in an unprecedented display of unity. This occasion was an **auspicious** beginning to the new South Africa. It marked an end to the **iniquitous** system of apartheid, which was intended systematically to oppress all nonwhites.

Under apartheid rule, democracy was seriously **abridged** and only whites—who made up just 12 percent of the population—had the right to vote and serve in political office. As a result, the laws that were passed were biased against the black majority.

Nelson Mandela grew up under the apartheid system. His birth name was Rolihlahla Mandela, but the name Nelson was given to him in school, where all black students were given English names. Mandela saw nothing objectionable about this custom. He was **inured** to the unjust system of apartheid when he was young and was unaware that there was any other way. But over time, as he heard black speakers lash out at the government and its policies, he increasingly began to question the system. Then his friend and **confidant**, Walter Sisulu, got him interested in political activism with the African National Congress.

The African National Congress (ANC) began as a political organization of mainly middle-class **constituents** who sought to end the social inequalities in South Africa through nonviolent means. In 1944, Mandela joined the ANC and became one of the organization's leading figures. He was one of the founders of the Youth League, a subgroup designed to broaden the organization's membership in an effort to mobilize more blacks. ANC membership increased significantly in the 1950s, during which time the organization put forth its Freedom Charter, which stated that "South Africa belongs to all who live in it, black and white."

After the 1960 massacre of hundreds of unarmed anti-apartheid protesters in the **beleaguered** black community of Sharpeville, the ANC became increasingly militant and began a campaign of **sabotage** against the government. Soon afterward, the government outlawed the ANC, along with all other black political organizations. In 1964, Mandela was sentenced to life in prison for his ANC involvement.

In prison, Mandela was given little food, was forced to do hard labor, and was only allowed two visitors and two letters a year. He continued his work as an ANC activist along with other imprisoned ANC members, but communication was difficult because he and his cohorts were almost always under the watchful eyes of prison guards. To make matters worse, some of the prison guards were particularly **sadistic** and worked to make prison life even more difficult. However, despite such hardships, Mandela bore no **animosity** toward his captors. Instead, he remained committed to his cause for freedom and kept his spirits strong. As Mandela states in his autobiography, *Long Walk to Freedom*, "Strong convictions are the secret of surviving deprivation."

In 1976, student protesters **inveighing** against apartheid policies were massacred in the black township of Soweto. The **abominable** treatment of the demonstrators motivated a resurgence of young black activism. As the government became increasingly oppressive, pressure mounted against it and its system of apartheid. Not only did protests increase, but **scathing** criticisms of South Africa's apartheid policies became widespread in the international community. Several countries showed their opposition by limiting their business with South Africa, which led to economic hardship for the country.

In response to the rising pressure, a series of momentous events **transpired**. In 1990 and 1991, the government lifted its ban on the ANC, released Mandela, and nullified the basic apartheid laws. Mandela was elected the new president of the ANC, and he and de Klerk began negotiating for a new constitution that would give equal rights to all citizens. The first all-races elections were held in April 1994; Mandela was elected president of South Africa.

He successfully oversaw the difficult transition of his country from an apartheid state to a free one and helped improve the lives of most South Africans, but the long journey toward social equality is not finished. It will be up to his successors to continue undoing the legacy of apartheid in the years ahead.

Answer each of the following questions in the form of a sentence. If a question does not contain a vocabulary word from this lesson's word list, use one in your answer. Use each word only once.

1. Who is F. W. de Klerk?

2. Why does the passage refer to the system of apartheid as **iniquitous**?

3. How was democracy **abridged** during apartheid rule?

4. Why didn't Mandela complain about being given an English name at school?

5. Who is Walter Sisulu?

6. Why was the Youth League started?

7. When did the ANC begin its campaign of **sabotage** against the government?

8. What is some evidence that Mandela kept his spirits strong during his incarceration?

abominate
abridge
animosity
auspicious
beleaguer
confidant
constituent
iniquitous
inure
inveigh
predecessor
sabotage
sadistic
scathing
transpire

9. What event in the 1970s inspired a resurgence of young black activism?

10. What **transpired** because of the escalating pressure against apartheid?

FUN & FASCINATING FACTS

In 1887, relations in France between workers and their bosses reached a historic low. In an attempt to get their bosses to change unacceptable working conditions, workers disrupted their company's production. One method they used was to jam their wooden shoes, called *sabots*, into the machinery, causing considerable damage to it. The word **sabotage** is derived from this period.

Confidant and **confident** are different words that are easily confused. **Confidant** is a noun; *confident* is an adjective.

Lesson 16

Word List
Study the definitions of the words below; then do the exercises for the lesson.

aura
ôr´ ə

n. A distinctive atmosphere or feeling that seems to surround someone or something; a distinctive appearance or impression.
There was an **aura** of serenity about the woman sitting quietly in the corner.

banal
bā´ nəl

adj. Lacking freshness; trite.
The plot of that movie was so **banal**, I predicted the ending within the first half hour.

bemuse
bi myo͞oz´

v. To confuse or bewilder.
The noise and hubbub of Times Square **bemused** the tourists, who had come from a rural area for their first trip to New York City.

cognizant
käg´ ni zənt

adj. Fully aware; taking notice.
Janine was so mesmerized by the clown at the fair that she was not **cognizant** of her surroundings.
cognizance *n.*
He did not take **cognizance** of the fact that Grossman's had closed, even though he passed by the store every day.

conundrum
kə nun´ drəm

n. 1. A riddle whose answer is a play on words.
Answer this **conundrum**: "What's the difference between an engineer and a professor?" "One minds trains and the other trains minds."
2. A puzzle or problem that is difficult or impossible to solve.
How Giovanna would be able to live in Turkey for three months without knowing a word of the language was a **conundrum** we could not solve.

evanescent
ev ə nes´ ənt

adj. Short-lived; staying temporarily.
Evening showers are an **evanescent** phenomenon in the tropics.

factotum
fak tōt´ əm

n. A helper or assistant with a wide range of duties and responsibilities.
The studio head made the decisions, and his **factotum** handled the details.

grandiose
gran´ dē ōs

adj. 1. Impressive because of large size or scope.
Gothic cathedrals are **grandiose** structures that continue to attract tourists.
2. Characterized by the pretense of grandeur or absurd exaggeration.
He made the **grandiose** claim that he was the only person in the world who could do the job.

induce
in do͞os´

v. 1. To influence or persuade.
We finally **induced** my grandmother to use the air conditioner we put in her bedroom.
2. To bring about; to cause.
That medication **induces** drowsiness, so it's unwise to drive after taking it.

intransigent
in tran´ sə jənt

adj. Refusing to compromise or change one's position on an issue.
The new committee's **intransigent** attitude made it impossible to work out any sort of compromise with the veteran employees.
intransigence *n.*
Because of her **intransigence** her friends gave up trying to persuade her to apply to more than one college.

laudatory
lôd´ ə tôr ē

adj. Full of praise.
A **laudatory** review in the *St. Louis Post-Dispatch* guaranteed a successful run for the new play.

panache
pə näsh´

n. Dash or flamboyance in style or action.
The chef chopped and diced the vegetables with awe-inspiring **panache**.

picayune
pik´ ə yōōn

adj. Petty or insignificant; concerned with trifling matters.
When evaluating the house, the inspector looked at the most **picayune** details, practically checking every nail and splinter.

predilection
pred əl ek´ shən

n. An inclination; preference.
I have a **predilection** for Thai food and eat it at least once a week.

promontory
präm´ ən tôr ē

n. A high point of land that juts out into water.
We had a beautiful view of the whole surrounding bay from the rocky **promontory**.

16A Understanding Meanings

Read the sentences below. If a sentence correctly uses the word in bold, write *C* on the line below it. If a sentence is incorrect, rewrite it so that the vocabulary word in bold is used correctly.

1. A **predilection** is a statement of what will happen in the future.

_____

2. A **factotum** is a fact whose truth is called into question.

_____

3. A **grandiose** scheme is one whose merits are greatly exaggerated.

_____

4. To be **cognizant** of something is to have no knowledge of it.

_____

5. A **banal** poem is one that lacks originality or flair.

_____

6. To **induce** someone to act is to persuade that person to act.

_____

7. A **bemused** expression indicates pleasure or enjoyment.

8. A **laudatory** comment is one that offers a warning.

9. If someone is **evanescent,** that person is unwilling to give in.

10. A **promontory** is a piece of land completely surrounded by water.

11. A **conundrum** is a question whose answer makes a play on words.

12. An **intransigent** person is one who stubbornly refuses to yield.

13. A **picayune** matter is one that requires much deliberation.

14. An **aura** is a distinct period of time in history.

15. **Panache** is a certain flair with which something is done.

aura
banal
bemuse
cognizant
conundrum
evanescent
factotum
grandiose
induce
intransigent
laudatory
panache
picayune
predilection
promontory

16B Using Words

If the word (or a form of the word) in bold fits in a sentence in the group below it, write the word in the blank. If the word does not fit, leave the space empty.

1. **factotum**

   (a) The story he told you is a _____ without a shred of truth to it.

   (b) The general's _____ had helped him out for nearly thirty years.

   (c) Jasper carried a little carved _____ , which he claimed brought him luck.

2. **intransigent**

   (a) These goods are _____ and are not to be shipped out of the warehouse.

   (b) If both parties keep being so _____ , it will be impossible to reach an agreement.

   (c) It seems he is now starting to modify his previously _____ attitude.

3. **cognizant**

   (a) Since I am not _____ of all the facts, I will reserve comment until later.

   (b) I remembered her face at once, but I was not _____ of her name.

   (c) He was not _____ of the fact that the dog was lying on the couch and he almost sat on her.

4. **promontory**

   (a) The lighthouse had been built at the end of the rocky _____ .

   (b) He had a sudden _____ that all was not well with his friend.

   (c) The _____ note you signed is now due and must be paid in full.

5. **aura**

   (a) The family's _____ of respectability was dissipated by the scandal.

   (b) He carried an _____ made of gold as a symbol of his office.

   (c) There was an _____ of greatness about him that impressed even his enemies.

6. **picayune**

   (a) It's surprising that those two close friends are still fighting over such a _____ matter.

   (b) To that billionaire, a thousand dollars seemed _____ .

   (c) He seemed to behave more _____ than ever as he got older.

7. **panache**

   (a) She dresses with such _____ .

   (b) The painter never quite recaptured the _____ of her earlier works.

   (c) Vasquez traveled in a fine _____ drawn by four jet black horses.

8. induce

(a) The rotating magnets _____ an electric current in the copper wire.

(b) She was skeptical at first, but I _____ her to give the product a try.

(c) Ty Cobb was one of the first players _____ into the Baseball Hall of Fame.

16C Word Study

Complete the analogies by selecting the pair of words whose relationship most resembles the relationship of the pair in capital letters. Circle the letter in front of the pair you choose.

1. AMBIVALENCE : CERTITUDE ::
   (a) imbalance : equilibrium
   (b) exodus : departure
   (c) restriction : restraint
   (d) rancor : acrimony

2. ABRIDGE : NOVEL ::
   (a) adjudicate : contest
   (b) compose : tune
   (c) recite : poem
   (d) crop : photograph

3. DIFFICULT : INTRACTABLE ::
   (a) voluntary : mandatory
   (b) unruly : rambunctious
   (c) smooth : slippery
   (d) ephemeral : permanent

4. COLLECT : DISBURSE ::
   (a) commit : perpetrate
   (b) dissipate : permeate
   (c) improve : ameliorate
   (d) mitigate : aggravate

5. CELESTIAL : SKY ::
   (a) stalwart : supporter
   (b) sunny : weather
   (c) agrarian : farm
   (d) diminutive : replica

6. STAR : GALAXY ::
   (a) snowflake : snowball
   (b) epitaph : tombstone
   (c) wave : ocean
   (d) universe : earth

7. BELIE : CONTRADICT ::
   (a) countenance : forbid
   (b) expedite : hasten
   (c) berate : praise
   (d) instigate : investigate

8. BENEVOLENCE : ANIMOSITY ::
   (a) accolade : rebuke
   (b) salary : stipend
   (c) follower : cohort
   (d) instruction : tutelage

9. CURTAIL : ERADICATE ::
   (a) evaporate : dissipate
   (b) harm : destroy
   (c) improve : exacerbate
   (d) help : hinder

aura
banal
bemuse
cognizant
conundrum
evanescent
factotum
grandiose
induce
intransigent
laudatory
panache
picayune
predilection
promontory

10. DISLIKE : ABOMINATE ::

(a) freeze : liquidate   (c) respect : adulate

(b) forbid : condone   (d) obey : flout

16D Images of Words

Circle the letter of each sentence that suggests the numbered bold vocabulary word. In each group, you may circle more than one letter or none at all.

1. **bemused**

   (a) As Jory stared at her long-lost brother, she could barely believe her eyes.

   (b) When we flipped on the lights and yelled "Surprise!", Margaret was at a loss for words.

   (c) Carmine's rendition of *Green Eggs and Ham* had everyone in fits of laughter.

2. **evanescent**

   (a) Many pop singers have one or two hits and then disappear from the charts forever.

   (b) The glow from the strange object increased as we stood watching it.

   (c) Most species of butterfly have a life span of less than a month.

3. **conundrum**

   (a) Which came first, the chicken or the egg?

   (b) Steve and Sandy had a horrible time trying to figure out how to get their huge sofa up the narrow, winding staircase.

   (c) Why do people picnic at the beach? Because of the sand which is there.

4. **picayune**

   (a) He agreed with the candidate's views, but he didn't vote for her because of her hairstyle.

   (b) The dish was made of chicken and noodles served with a hot and spicy sauce.

   (c) The biologists needed millions of dollars to fund their work in cancer research.

5. **intransigence**

   (a) A fallen tree blocked the road, making it impossible for us to continue.

   (b) The car wouldn't start because the battery was dead.

   (c) No matter what I said she wouldn't change her mind.

6. **cognizant**

   (a) Adrienne played field hockey every Saturday.

   (b) Letitia and Mason got along very well while working on their school project.

   (c) Luke was attentive to every detail in the painting at the museum.

7. **grandiose**

(a) Sam claimed that he was the most talented musician in the country.

(b) His plan to swim across the Atlantic is ambitious.

(c) Shannon's offer to pay for lunch was very generous.

8. **predilection**

(a) Tomorrow's weather is expected to be warm and sunny with a light breeze.

(b) The artist liked to use mostly earth tones and avoided bright, primary colors.

(c) She would read only Victorian novels.

9. **laudatory**

(a) Casey seems to have a very high opinion of himself.

(b) This year's basketball team is the best in the school's history.

(c) Kendra's parents congratulated her for raising her grade point average from a C- to a B+.

10. **panache**

(a) She acted as though breaking the world's high jump record was no big deal.

(b) The actor's grace and flair made it clear he loved to perform for a live audience.

(c) My aunt likes to wear stylish hats with curling feathers.

16E Passage

Read the passage below; then complete the exercise that follows it.

Would You Like It Wrapped?

In part as a rebellion against art's consumer orientation, a movement known as "earth art" or "earthworks" developed in the 1960s. "Earth artists" set out to oppose the buying and selling of art by creating outdoor works that were either too big or too **evanescent** to own. For example, Walter De Maria's *Lightning Field* consists of 400 metal rods placed in a grid spanning thousands of square feet in an open field to attract lightning, and Robert Smithson's *Spiral Jetty*—a spiral dirt path that leads into Utah's Great Salt Lake—has been submerged by natural flooding.

Arguably the most famous earth artist is a man named Christo, born Christo Vladimirov Javacheff in Bulgaria in 1935. Before settling in New York, Christo studied at the Art Academy in Bulgaria and the Fine Arts Academy in Austria, and worked in Paris, where he met his wife, Jeanne-Claude. Originally his **factotum**, Jeanne-Claude is now his trusted advisor and collaborator on earthworks.

Christo is known for his **predilection** for wrapping large objects. His earlier works involved wrapping **banal** objects such as road signs, bicycles, and chairs. In the sixties, before he gained widespread popularity, Christo had grander visions, such as wrapping a school and a couple of landmarks around Paris, but the French government would not permit it. As his public acceptance grew, however, Christo was allowed to wrap buildings in several cities around the world. Over time, some of Christo's works have escalated to such a scale that his earlier projects seem insignificant in comparison. For example, Christo wrapped several islands off the coast of Miami in bright pink plastic (1983), Paris's famous Pont-Neuf bridge in gold fabric (1985), and an entire **promontory** on the Australian coastline in white fabric (1987).

aura
banal
bemuse
cognizant
conundrum
evanescent
factotum
grandiose
induce
intransigent
laudatory
panache
picayune
predilection
promontory

Because of the grand scale of Christo's earthworks, figuring out how to execute them can be a **conundrum** for workers. Completing a work often involves hiring a crew to erect his extraordinary pieces as well as battling courts, environmentalists, and neighboring residents to get permission to carry out his projects. For example, his work *Running Fence*, a white nylon fence that extended for twenty-four miles in California, took thirteen years of preparation before it was completed in 1976. Christo and his wife had to **induce** sixty landowners and fifteen government bodies to give their permission, attend seventeen public hearings, file a 450-page environmental impact report, and deal with objections ranging from the most thoughtful to the most **picayune**.

In addition, the people who lived in the area were quite skeptical: "I've been hanging laundry for sixty years and nobody's ever called me an artist," remarked a **bemused** resident. The most **intransigent** opposition came from local artists who claimed the project was a publicity stunt that would give art a bad name. The reviews, however, were **laudatory**: one critic commented that "*Running Fence* . . . is not only a piece of sculpture but itself sculpts the land."

On February 12, 2005, Christo and Jeanne-Claude unveiled *The Gates* in New York's Central Park. In the days before the opening, six hundred workers installed 7,500 sixteen-foot-tall gates stretched out along twenty-three miles of Central Park's walkways. Over one million square feet of saffron-colored fabric was used to create the panels, which moved with the wind. The changing light turned the panels from golden-yellow to deep red against the wintry, gray background of the park. *The Gates* was designed to be temporary: it stood for only sixteen days, then the materials were recycled. During that time, millions of visitors had the chance to enjoy this bright ribbon on the dark winter landscape.

Christo's work is controversial. But while some are skeptical, many fans and critics believe that his work has **panache** and provides an **aura** of mystery and whimsy. Christo himself claims that his art is more than just frivolity; he believes it has social significance. His fanciful and dramatic alterations to environments and landmarks are an effort to encourage people to consider their relationship both to his works and to the immediate environment, thereby urging spectators to be newly **cognizant** of the meaning of setting.

The most **grandiose** project of all is still only a gleam in Christo's eye. He would like to erect a series of glass walls, temporarily blocking off all east–west traffic across the United States. It is unlikely that even Christo will be able to accomplish this feat.

Answer each of the following questions in the form of a sentence. If a question does not contain a vocabulary word from this lesson's word list, use one in your answer. Use each word only once.

1. Would you agree with an art critic who called Christo's work **banal**? Why or why not?

2. What kinds of things might Jeanne-Claude have done when she first worked with Christo?

3. Why does Christo intend his projects to be **evanescent**?

4. What would be an example of a **picayune** objection to *Running Fence?*

5. What was Christo's work on the Australian coastline?

6. Why might figuring out how to implement one of Christo's earthworks be a **conundrum**?

7. Name one of the things Christo and his wife had to do to begin working on *Running Fence*.

8. Was the critic quoted in the passage an **intransigent** opponent of *Running Fence*?

9. Does Christo have an artistic goal beyond the purely aesthetic?

10. What type of project does Christo seem to prefer?

FUN & FASCINATING FACTS

A **picayune** was a five-cent coin that was formerly used in Louisiana. Its low value gave rise to the saying, "not worth a picayune," which led to its current meaning.

The Latin *laudare* means "to praise," and the English verb *laud*, which has the same meaning, is derived from it. Two related adjectives have quite different meanings: **laudatory** means "expressing praise." (The governor handed out many accolades during his *laudatory* address.) *Laudable* means "worthy of praise." (Even though they failed, they made a *laudable* effort).

Review for Lessons 13–16

Hidden Message In the boxes provided, write the words from Lessons 13 through 16 that are missing in each of the sentences below. The number following each sentence gives the word list from which the missing word must be taken. When the exercise is finished, the shaded boxes will spell out an observation by the British statesman Winston S. Churchill.

1. The facts explain but do not _____ the offense. (13)

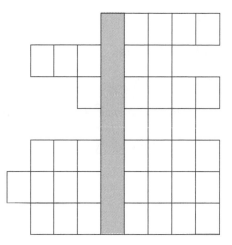

2. You must face the consequences if you _____ the rules. (13)

3. The _____ contains two hundred million stars. (14)

4. We became _____ to hardship during those years. (15)

5. He had a(n) _____ of happiness. (16)

6. Her _____ usually makes all the arrangements. (16)

7. My _____ would never betray my trust. (15)

8. At this _____ the parties agreed to disagree. (14)

9. You were _____ in not calling the doctor at once. (14)

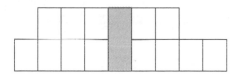

10. Something will _____ to change her opinion. (15)

11. The _____ extends a mile into the water. (16)

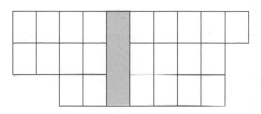

12. I defy anyone to solve this _____ . (16)

13. What _____ did he use in order to deceive you? (13)

14. Susan B. Anthony was a(n) _____ advocate of women's rights. (13)

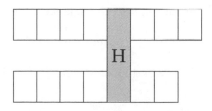

15. The press continues to _____ him for his mistakes. (14)

16. Nothing could _____ her to leave her home. (16)

17. We will _____ the pictures to compare them. (14)

18. The hurricane's _____ force caused considerable damage. (14)

19. The plot to _____ the installation was foiled. (15)

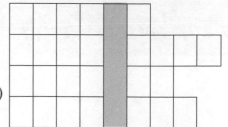

20. These matters are too _____ to concern us. (16)

21. The magician performed his tricks with _____ . (16)

22. A license is _____ in order to fish in the lake. (13)

23. Andrew's _____ voice almost put me to sleep. (13)

24. The aliens' visit was a _____ occurrence. (13)

25. Unfortunately, the facts _____ his story. (13)

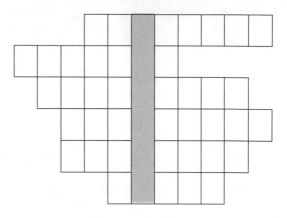

26. Our genes comprise many _____ elements. (13)

27. A solar eclipse is a spectacular _____ sight. (14)

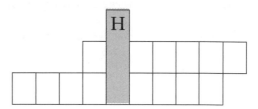

28. She keeps the car tuned for _____ performance. (14)
29. He predicted the outcome of the game with absolute _____ . (14)

30. It is useless to _____ against the terrible weather. (15)

31. My new assistant is much more organized than her _____ . (15)

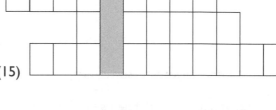

32. Her teacher's _____ recommendation helped Lara get accepted into the science program. (16)

33. Dawn's _____ lecture bored the audience. (16)

34. This weed-killer should _____ the crabgrass on your lawn. (13)

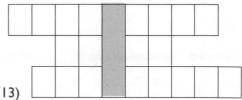

W

35. I bear him no _____ despite his churlish ways. (15)

36. Lauren has _____ dreams of single-handedly putting an end to poverty in the United States. (16)

37. The politician publicly thanked his _____ for their votes. (15)

38. The problem seemed _____ at first. (14)

H

39. The _____ in the lens is easily corrected. (14)

40. I am quite _____ of the difficulties involved. (16)

41. The artist illustrates the _____ of battle. (13)

42. He spoke sadly of the _____ beauty of youth. (16)

43. The _____ occurs where two rivers meet. (14)

44. The principal administered a(n) _____ rebuke. (15)

45. Fred's weak denial left his parents _____ . (16)

46. Who will _____ the charitable trust's funds? (14)

47. Though _____ , the machine still works well. (14)

48. Sometimes people _____ others for expressing unpopular opinions. (15)

49. The department is a(n) _____ to the ministry. (13)

50. The two choices present me with a(n) _____ . (13)

51. The agreement is a(n) _____ event. (15)

52. These reports _____ distrust of our leaders. (13)

Lesson 17

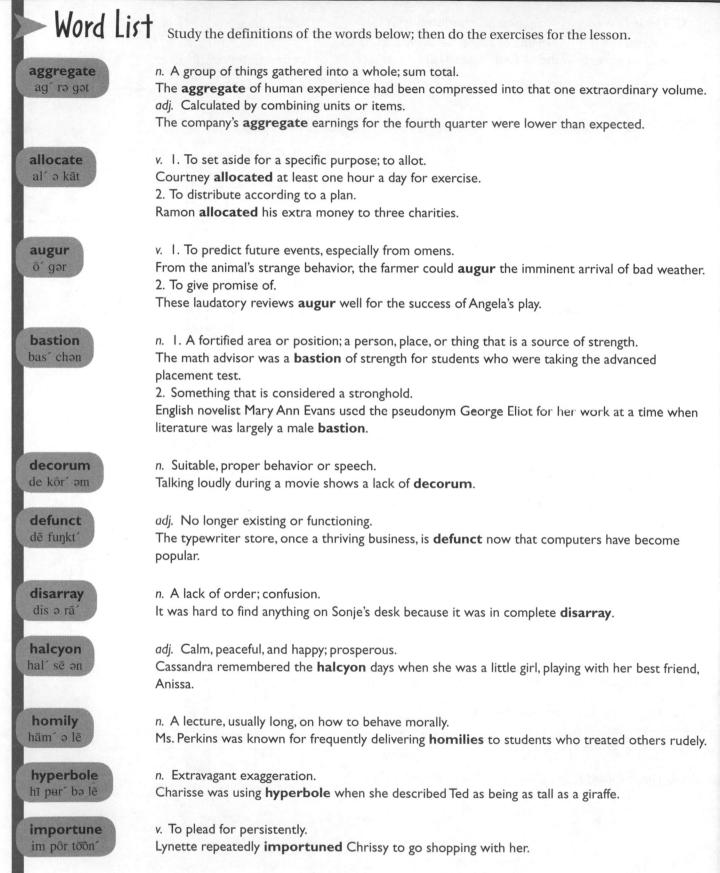

> **Word List** Study the definitions of the words below; then do the exercises for the lesson.

aggregate
ag´ rə gət

n. A group of things gathered into a whole; sum total.
The **aggregate** of human experience had been compressed into that one extraordinary volume.
adj. Calculated by combining units or items.
The company's **aggregate** earnings for the fourth quarter were lower than expected.

allocate
al´ ə kāt

v. 1. To set aside for a specific purpose; to allot.
Courtney **allocated** at least one hour a day for exercise.
2. To distribute according to a plan.
Ramon **allocated** his extra money to three charities.

augur
ô´ gər

v. 1. To predict future events, especially from omens.
From the animal's strange behavior, the farmer could **augur** the imminent arrival of bad weather.
2. To give promise of.
These laudatory reviews **augur** well for the success of Angela's play.

bastion
bas´ chən

n. 1. A fortified area or position; a person, place, or thing that is a source of strength.
The math advisor was a **bastion** of strength for students who were taking the advanced placement test.
2. Something that is considered a stronghold.
English novelist Mary Ann Evans used the pseudonym George Eliot for her work at a time when literature was largely a male **bastion**.

decorum
de kôr´ əm

n. Suitable, proper behavior or speech.
Talking loudly during a movie shows a lack of **decorum**.

defunct
dē fuŋkt´

adj. No longer existing or functioning.
The typewriter store, once a thriving business, is **defunct** now that computers have become popular.

disarray
dis ə rā´

n. A lack of order; confusion.
It was hard to find anything on Sonje's desk because it was in complete **disarray**.

halcyon
hal´ sē ən

adj. Calm, peaceful, and happy; prosperous.
Cassandra remembered the **halcyon** days when she was a little girl, playing with her best friend, Anissa.

homily
häm´ ə lē

n. A lecture, usually long, on how to behave morally.
Ms. Perkins was known for frequently delivering **homilies** to students who treated others rudely.

hyperbole
hī pur´ bə lē

n. Extravagant exaggeration.
Charisse was using **hyperbole** when she described Ted as being as tall as a giraffe.

importune
im pôr tōōn´

v. To plead for persistently.
Lynette repeatedly **importuned** Chrissy to go shopping with her.

jurisdiction
joor is dik´ shən

n. Legal authority to govern or control.
The federal government has **jurisdiction** over the nation's air traffic control system.

ruminate
roo´ mə nāt

v. To think over again and again; to ponder.
I spent weeks **ruminating** about the meaning of Kafka's novella *Metamorphosis*.
rumination *n.* The act of pondering; reflection.
Einstein's **ruminations** led him to challenge common perceptions of time and space.

temerity
tə mer´ ə tē

n. Reckless boldness without regard to danger or opposition.
Desmond did not have the **temerity** to correct the French teacher's faulty pronunciation.

winnow
win´ ō

v. To separate and remove what is undesirable and leave what is desirable; to blow away the chaff from grain.
It was Nadia's job to interview potential employees, **winnow** out the unqualified candidates, and recommend the qualified candidates for a second interview.

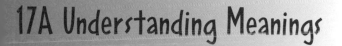

17A Understanding Meanings

Read the sentences below. If a sentence correctly uses the word in bold, write *C* on the line below it. If a sentence is incorrect, rewrite it so that the vocabulary word in bold is used correctly.

1. To **ruminate** over something is to think deeply about it.

2. To have **jurisdiction** over something is to have legal authority over it.

3. A **defunct** organization is one that functions as part of a larger group.

4. To act with **temerity** is to act with a reckless disregard for negative consequences.

5. To **winnow** grain is to separate the wheat from the chaff.

6. To **allocate** funds is to receive them for some worthwhile purpose.

7. The **aggregate** of things is the collection of them.

8. A **homily** is a brief saying that contains much wisdom.

9. A **bastion** is something that serves as a source of protection.

10. To **importune** someone is to pester that person for something.

11. **Decorum** is proper behavior.

12. A **halcyon** era is one that seems to have been happy and peaceful.

13. To **augur** something is to foretell its occurrence.

14. To be in **disarray** is to be in a state of disorder.

15. To engage in **hyperbole** is to act agitated or nervous.

aggregate
allocate
augur
bastion
decorum
defunct
disarray
halcyon
homily
hyperbole
importune
jurisdiction
ruminate
temerity
winnow

17B Using Words

If the word (or a form of the word) in bold fits in a sentence in the group below it, write the word in the blank. If the word does not fit, leave the space empty.

1. **importune**

  (a) My little brother _____ me to take him to the puppet show until I gave in.

  (b) This is an _____ time to bring up such a delicate matter.

  (c) Television commercials _____ viewers to Buy! Buy! Buy!

2. winnow

(a) It was my job to _____ out the errors in the thirty-two-page document.

(b) The filter _____ the lighter husks from the heavier grain.

(c) After we _____ out the author's prejudices from the facts in her article, we realized that she gave little firm support for her argument.

3. aggregate

(a) Eden _____ everyone at the meeting by insisting on doing things her way.

(b) Noel found the _____ of shirts sold by tallying up the amount of shirts customers ordered and deducting the number of shirts that were returned.

(c) Last year's theater ticket sales reached an _____ of almost fifty thousand dollars.

4. allocate

(a) We _____ a third of all income from sales for repairs to the building.

(b) How much time do you _____ for homework each evening?

(c) We need to _____ one of the rooms as a storage area.

5. disarray

(a) The candidate's unexpected withdrawal threw the election into _____ .

(b) Our class was _____ by the fire alarm.

(c) The organization was in a state of _____ until Ravi took it over.

6. augur

(a) Eight nominations for the Academy Awards _____ well for the movie's ticket sales.

(b) Tia couldn't decide whether she _____ appropriately at the formal party.

(c) The lack of funds and poor management _____ failure for the project.

7. homily

(a) The subject of the guest speaker's _____ was "How to do more with your time."

(b) The _____ of the story is "An ounce of prevention is worth a pound of cure."

(c) The annual charity event _____ drew a larger than average crowd this year.

8. halcyon

(a) The TV program looks back at the _____ era known as "television's golden age."

(b) The book brought back memories of Zach's _____ days visiting his grandparents.

(c) Jason was very angry with his sister and called her _____ names.

17C Word Study

Change each of the nouns below into an adjective by changing, adding, or dropping the suffix. Write the word in the space provided.

Noun	Adjective
1. tenacity	_____
2. axiom	_____
3. cataclysm	_____
4. catharsis	_____
5. cognizance	_____

Change each of the verbs below into a noun by changing, adding, or dropping the suffix. Write the word in the space provided.

Verb	Noun
6. concoct	_____
7. juxtapose	_____
8. constrain	_____
9. proliferate	_____
10. ruminate	_____

Change each of the adjectives below into a noun by changing, adding, or dropping the suffix. Write the word in the space provided.

Adjective	Noun
11. culpable	_____
12. diverse	_____
13. titanic	_____
14. grandiloquent	_____
15. intransigent	_____

aggregate
allocate
augur
bastion
decorum
defunct
disarray
halcyon
homily
hyperbole
importune
jurisdiction
ruminate
temerity
winnow

17D Images of Words

Circle the letter of each sentence that suggests the numbered bold vocabulary word. In each group, you may circle more than one letter or none at all.

1. **bastion**

   (a) Martin Luther King, Jr. and others kept the Civil Rights Movement going despite strong opposition.

   (b) For many years, military academies were able to exclude female students.

   (c) The Panama Canal, completed in 1914, connects the Atlantic and the Pacific oceans.

2. **homily**

   (a) The speaker regaled the audience with a string of amusing anecdotes.

   (b) The school principal lectured us on the importance of doing what is right.

   (c) "Drive carefully," Mother said as she gave me the keys to the car.

3. **jurisdiction**

   (a) I must have told Billy a hundred times to stay out of my room.

   (b) The Passport Office is a part of the State Department.

   (c) The Department of the Interior is responsible for all national parks.

4. **temerity**

   (a) A stranger came up to me and asked for a "loan" of a hundred dollars.

   (b) Holden was shaking with fear as he crossed the rope bridge high above the gorge.

   (c) Alexa tends to leap before she looks.

5. **decorum**

   (a) The room had been freshly painted and new drapes had been hung.

   (b) The tall sailing ships made a graceful entry into the harbor.

   (c) It's always a pleasure to go to Jamal's house for dinner because he's such a gracious host.

6. **hyperbole**

   (a) Whatever you've got in this box, it weighs a ton.

   (b) Janna is as slow as molasses.

   (c) While Joelle was waiting for news about her sister's operation, she couldn't sit still and paced constantly until the phone call came through.

7. **winnow**

   (a) Paolo made a list of all the food he needed for the party.

   (b) In less than a year, Nathan had spent his entire inheritance.

   (c) The moon was just a thin curved sliver in the night sky.

8. **ruminate**

(a) Nick couldn't stand all of Elijah's nagging.

(b) "I've been giving your proposal a great deal of thought," said Grandfather.

(c) The idea for the story had been on Sebastian's mind for some time.

9. **importune**

(a) Father reminded me to be sure to lock the front door when I came home.

(b) That salesperson trying to sell perfume refused to take no for an answer.

(c) Every day these tomatoes are flown into the country from Holland.

10. **defunct**

(a) Avery was so scared that he turned and ran as fast as his legs could carry him.

(b) After seventy years, the Soviet Union came to an end in the 1980s.

(c) The last issue of the magazine came out in May 1994.

17E Passage

Read the passage below; then complete the exercise that follows it.

The All-American Girls Professional Baseball League

Professional sports, long a male **bastion** in the United States, have been opening up to include more women. In 1997, two professional women's basketball leagues and a professional women's softball league were formed. In the 1998 Winter Olympics, women's ice hockey, snowboarding, and curling were all added to the games for the first time, as was women's wrestling for the 2004 games.

This growth in women's professional sports was preceded many years ago by a women's baseball league, the All-American Girls Professional Baseball League (AAGPBL). The AAGPBL came into existence in 1943, after the United States had become embroiled in World War II. With most minor league players drafted into the service and half of the major league players in military uniform, baseball was in **disarray**, and the 1943 season was in doubt. Philip Wrigley, owner of the Chicago Cubs, was **ruminating** in his office over the situation when an idea came to him: women were doing many of the jobs previously done only by men; perhaps they could play professional baseball, too.

Women's softball enjoyed great popularity at this time; in the Los Angeles area alone there were more than a thousand teams. Scouts began an intensive national search for the most talented players. From more than a hundred hopefuls who came to Chicago's Wrigley Field in 1943 for tryouts, they **winnowed** out sixty potential players. Fifteen players were **allocated** to each of the four teams in the new league: the Racine Belles and Kenosha Comets in Wisconsin, the South Bend Blue Sox in Indiana, and the Rockford Peaches in Illinois. The players were employed by the Wrigley organization, which initially had **jurisdiction** over all aspects of the league until ownership of each team was given to the town for which it played.

During the first season, paid attendance at AAGPBL games often exceeded 3,000, which **augured** well for the league's future. In addition, players' salaries were generous by the standards of the time. In 1943, the average working person's salary ranged from $10 to $20 a week; players were making between $45 and $85 dollars a week.

aggregate
allocate
augur
bastion
decorum
defunct
disarray
halcyon
homily
hyperbole
importune
jurisdiction
ruminate
temerity
winnow

In addition to playing baseball, players were required to be "feminine" and of "high moral standing." As a result, players were directed to wear lipstick during games, to make sure that their hair showed from under their baseball caps, and to wear skirts at all times when in public. Each team had a chaperone, who was hired to watch over the athletes and to deliver **homilies** in case any of the players had the **temerity** to violate the rules of **decorum**.

By 1948, the league had expanded to ten teams, and the **aggregate** of ticket sales for the season topped the one-million-dollar mark. The game got tougher over the years. In the beginning, a softball with a twelve-inch circumference was thrown underhand; by 1954, pitchers were throwing a standard nine-inch hardball overhand. Base path lengths and pitching distances also increased. The level of play was extremely high. Hall-of-Famer Max Carey, of the Pittsburgh Pirates, was not engaging in **hyperbole** when he stated that a 1946 game between the Rockford Peaches and the Racine Belles was "Barring none, even in the majors . . . the best game I've ever seen."

The televising of men's major league games in the early 1950s caused a sharp drop-off in attendance at AAGPBL games, and by the end of the 1954 season the league was **defunct**. The players went their separate ways, keeping alive the memory of those **halcyon** days by means of newsletters.

For years, few people remembered or knew of the existence of the AAGPBL. However, in the late 1980s, Frances Janssen, a former AAGPBL player with the Fort Wayne Daisies, worked with other former league players to **importune** the Baseball Hall of Fame for official recognition of the league. In 1988, the Baseball Hall of Fame officially recognized the league, and in 1992, a major motion picture, *A League of Their Own*, depicted the life of the league and some of its dominant players.

Answer each of the following questions in the form of a sentence. If a question does not contain a vocabulary word from this lesson's word list, use one in your answer. Use each word only once.

1. About how many women's softball teams were in existence around Los Angeles in the early 1940s?

2. Where did the idea for the AAGPBL come from?

3. How were players chosen at the Chicago tryouts?

4. Who eventually assumed control of the AAGPBL teams?

5. How does the passage suggest that a paid attendance of 3,000 was a good record for the first season of the AAGPBL?

6. What made the years of the AAGPBL a **halcyon** time for the players?

7. What might team chaperones **importune** their charges about?

8. What caused the AAGPBL to fall into **disarray** and what was the result?

9. Why does baseball owe a debt of gratitude to Frances Janssen?

10. What **bastion** did Frances Janssen challenge?

FUN & FASCINATING FACTS

In ancient Rome, priests who foretold the future were called *augurs*. They made their predictions by studying the internal organs of birds, by studying their flight, and by various other esoteric means. The word survives as the English verb **augur**, "to indicate future events."

The word **bastion** can be traced to the Old French word *bastillon*, which meant "a fortress." Over time, the word transformed into *bastille* and came to mean "a prison." The Bastille was the Paris prison stormed by a mob on July 14, 1789, at the onset of the French Revolution—a day that is still celebrated in France as Bastille Day.

Lesson 18

Word List
Study the definitions of the words below; then do the exercises for the lesson.

acoustic
ə kōōs´ tik

adj. Relating to sound or hearing.
A tiny **acoustic** device improved Grandfather's hearing.
acoustics *n.* The properties of an enclosed space that affect sound quality.
The pianist Martha Argerich checked the **acoustics** of the concert hall during her first practice session.

assemblage
ə sem´ blij

n. 1. A collection or gathering of people or things.
The **assemblage** at Camp Tamarack included people from all over the country.
2. A fitting together of parts.
A car engine is an **assemblage** of many parts working together.

august
ō gust´

adj. Inspiring great respect or admiration; noble.
Thomas Jefferson's **august** presence made a deep impression on those privileged to know him.

auspices
ôs´ pi səz

n. Protection, support, or guidance; patronage.
The concert is being given under the **auspices** of the town's arts foundation.

cavil
kav´ əl

v. To criticize unimportant things; to quibble.
Kara **caviled** at the majority vote to change the starting time of soccer practice from 3:30 to 3:45.
n. A minor criticism.
My only **cavil** with the restaurant is that they don't warm the bread.

curator
kyōōr´ āt ər

n. A person in charge of an exhibition; an overseer of a museum or library collection.
The **curator** wrote brief explanations for all the works in the Picasso exhibit.

extant
eks´ tənt

adj. Still existing; not lost or destroyed.
I had an opportunity to view one of the few **extant** copies of the first edition of *Middlemarch*.

gamut
gam´ ət

n. The entire range of something.
Stars run the **gamut** from Earth-sized white dwarfs to red giants, which are hundreds of times bigger than the sun.

ineffable
in ef´ ə bəl

adj. Incapable of being expressed in words.
They sat gazing at the **ineffable** beauty of the Green Mountains.

mellifluous
mə lif´ lōō əs

adj. Sweetly flowing; pleasant to the ear.
The **mellifluous** sound of a cello filled the rehearsal room.

mien
mēn

n. A person's manner, appearance, or expression; bearing.
Although Sandro was worried about all the work he had to do, you couldn't tell that from his untroubled **mien**.

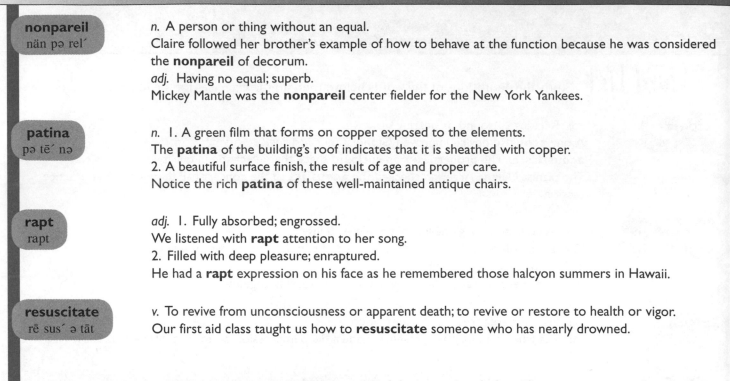

nonpareil
nän pə rel´

n. A person or thing without an equal.
Claire followed her brother's example of how to behave at the function because he was considered the **nonpareil** of decorum.
adj. Having no equal; superb.
Mickey Mantle was the **nonpareil** center fielder for the New York Yankees.

patina
pə tē´ nə

n. 1. A green film that forms on copper exposed to the elements.
The **patina** of the building's roof indicates that it is sheathed with copper.
2. A beautiful surface finish, the result of age and proper care.
Notice the rich **patina** of these well-maintained antique chairs.

rapt
rapt

adj. 1. Fully absorbed; engrossed.
We listened with **rapt** attention to her song.
2. Filled with deep pleasure; enraptured.
He had a **rapt** expression on his face as he remembered those halcyon summers in Hawaii.

resuscitate
rē sus´ ə tāt

v. To revive from unconsciousness or apparent death; to revive or restore to health or vigor.
Our first aid class taught us how to **resuscitate** someone who has nearly drowned.

18A Understanding Meanings

Read the sentences below. If a sentence correctly uses the word in bold, write *C* on the line below it. If a sentence is incorrect, rewrite it so that the vocabulary word in bold is used correctly.

1. An **ineffable** experience is one that words cannot adequately describe.

2. A **mellifluous** rendition is one that is pleasing to the ear.

3. **Acoustics** are the qualities of a space that determine how things sound.

4. The **auspices** of an organization refers to the support it lends.

5. A **cavil** is a major flaw.

acoustic
assemblage
august
auspices
cavil
curator
extant
gamut
ineffable
mellifluous
mien
nonpareil
patina
rapt
resuscitate

6. Someone's **mien** is that person's hopes and dreams.

7. A **rapt** expression is one of extreme boredom.

8. An **assemblage** is something put together from various parts.

9. To **resuscitate** an area is to bring it back to its former healthy state.

10. A **nonpareil** is a person who stands high above the rest.

11. An **august** figure is one that is revered.

12. An **extant** group is one that no longer exists.

13. A **patina** is a green coating formed on iron surfaces.

14. A **curator** is a person in charge of a museum collection.

15. To run the **gamut** is to span the entire range of something.

18B Using Words

If the word (or a form of the word) in bold fits in a sentence in the group below it, write the word in the blank. If the word does not fit, leave the space empty.

1. **ineffable**

   (a) A look of _____ joy crossed Tanya's face as they brought in her birthday cake.

   (b) The astronaut spoke of the _____ experience she had traveling in outer space.

   (c) The dry cleaner told us that the stain on the coat was _____ .

2. **curator**

   (a) The _____ of the museum's Egyptian collection arranged the exhibition.

   (b) The crown jewels were displayed in a bullet-proof glass _____ .

   (c) The _____ of the convenience store said she might have a job for me.

3. **mien**

   (a) The refined _____ of the stranger suggested he was of aristocratic birth.

   (b) The ambassador had the world-weary _____ of one who has seen everything.

   (c) The store's _____ is that all customers must be completely satisfied, or they get a full refund.

4. **resuscitate**

   (a) Vaudeville is defunct and attempts to _____ it are bound to fail.

   (b) The lifeguards were able to _____ the unconscious swimmer.

   (c) It cost about ten thousand dollars to _____ the building after the fire.

5. **august**

   (a) Lincoln's likeness is enshrined in the memorial bearing his _____ .

   (b) The archbishop's _____ manner did not encourage familiarity.

   (c) An _____ is a clown with a big red nose and curly orange wig.

6. **extant**

   (a) The last of the dinosaurs became _____ sixty-five million years ago.

   (b) This is one of the very few _____ Stanley Steamer cars in private hands.

   (c) The number of _____ diners grows smaller with each passing year.

7. **gamut**

   (a) The store has a _____ of men's suits on sale this month.

   (b) The _____ of visible light ranges from red to violet.

   (c) Ben's acting roles ran the _____ from comic minor parts to serious lead ones.

acoustic

assemblage

august

auspices

cavil

curator

extant

gamut

ineffable

mellifluous

mien

nonpareil

patina

rapt

resuscitate

8. **rapt**

   (a) Valeria's little sister had a _____ look on her face when the circus clown spoke to her.

   (b) Josie remained _____ in her studies and scarcely looked up when her friends came in.

   (c) The baby was _____ in a silk shawl that was passed down from her grandmother.

18C Word Study

Each group of four words below contains two words that are either synonyms or antonyms. Circle these two words; then circle the *S* if they are synonyms, the *A* if they are antonyms.

1. cognizant	culpable	laudatory	unaware	S	A
2. rapt	modest	esoteric	grandiose	S	A
3. quest	promontary	puzzle	conundrum	S	A
4. amused	bemused	intransigent	perplexed	S	A
5. jurisdiction	caution	honesty	temerity	S	A
6. interference	disarray	confusion	penchant	S	A
7. deny	allocate	distribute	importune	S	A
8. winnow	suggest	ruminate	sift	S	A
9. mellifluous	gossamer	extant	harsh	S	A
10. cavil	quibble	deny	resuscitate	S	A

18D Images of Words

Circle the letter of each sentence that suggests the numbered bold vocabulary word. In each group, you may circle more than one letter or none at all.

1. **cavil**

   (a) They will probably complain if the pizza arrives two minutes later than promised.

   (b) The mule just stood there and stubbornly refused to move forward.

   (c) Fiona believes firmly that all people deserve equal rights.

2. **mellifluous**

    (a) A calm, beautiful melody lulled them to sleep.

    (b) The drums beat a thunderous pulse as the marching band advanced.

    (c) The sound of the brook splashing over rocks was music to Carly's ears.

3. **patina**

    (a) The protective shield covering a turtle's back is called a carapace.

    (b) Its great age had not diminished the mahogany table's lustrous surface.

    (c) Michael's skin was as smooth as a baby's.

4. **assemblage**

    (a) The 1995 "Million Man March" on Washington was a very orderly affair that involved several hundred thousand men from around the United States.

    (b) It is difficult to tell the fake Rembrandt painting from the genuine one.

    (c) Every five years the Martines had a huge family gathering.

5. **auspices**

    (a) The local poetry society sponsored the competition.

    (b) The island of Guam was occupied by the Japanese during World War II.

    (c) The World Health Organization is an agency supported by the United Nations.

6. **resuscitate**

    (a) The only item not sold at the yard sale was an old, rickety chair.

    (b) The old abandoned mill was given new life after it was renovated to become a local arts center.

    (c) An electric shock started the patient's heart again after it had stopped beating.

7. **acoustics**

    (a) The panels behind the orchestra reflect sound into the auditorium.

    (b) Eli loves to sing in the shower because of the enhanced sound the tiles create.

    (c) Concertgoers declare there are no bad seats in Carnegie Hall.

8. **august**

    (a) The wind occasionally reached speeds of sixty-five miles an hour.

    (b) The parade took over an hour to pass the reviewing stand.

    (c) The rocks of the Canadian Shield are the oldest in North America.

9. **nonpareil**

    (a) Many believe that Minnesota Fats was the world's greatest pool player.

    (b) Africa's mightiest waterway is the world's longest river, the 4,134-mile-long Nile.

    (c) Rochelle prefers Harley-Davidson to any other motorcycle maker.

acoustic
assemblage
august
auspices
cavil
curator
extant
gamut
ineffable
mellifluous
mien
nonpareil
patina
rapt
resuscitate

10. **rapt**

(a) Members of the audience gave the soloist their close and undivided attention.

(b) I read the book without a break, completely unaware of what was going on around me.

(c) Tad was staring out the classroom window, a faraway look in his eyes.

18E Passage

Read the passage below; then complete the exercise that follows it.

The Violins of Cremona

Stringed instruments have existed for thousands of years. The oldest records and specimens of these musical instruments come from ancient Egypt and Mesopotamia (territory in present-day Iraq), and these include examples that run the **gamut** from the guitar and the ukulele to the harp and the piano. However, the violin, which is one of the most widely used instruments in the world, didn't emerge until after the Middle Ages. No one person is credited with creating the violin, but its development is rooted in northern Italy during the 16th century, when many violin makers were trying to master its creation. Many of the most famous violin makers came from one place—Cremona, Italy.

The Amati family began making stringed instruments in Cremona in the late 1500s; it was a pupil of this family, Antonio Stradivari, who is said to have perfected the violin about a hundred years later. Few masters of the violin would **cavil** at the proposition that, among violin makers, Stradivari is the **nonpareil**. Over a long and productive lifetime, he created more than a thousand instruments, of which perhaps two-thirds are **extant**. He was still busy in his workshop when he died in 1737, at the age of ninety-three.

If Stradivari had a rival—and most experts would maintain that he does not—that person is Giuseppe Guarneri. Also a native of Cremona, he was born in 1698, fifty-four years after Stradivari. His output was smaller than Stradivari's, with an estimated one hundred of his violins still surviving. It is said that a Stradivarius gives a pure, silvery tone that stimulates an aristocratic **mien** in the violinist, while a Guarnerius has an earthier, less **august** tone. Violinist Kyung-Wha Chung, who uses a Guarnerius, likens playing it to "feeling the dirt under your feet."

The **ineffable** sound qualities of Stradivarius and Guarnerius violins have not been reproduced in any other violins made since. Typically, the body of a violin is constructed from an **assemblage** of about seventy small pieces of wood glued together. It's known that Stradivari and Guarneri used softwood such as spruce or pine for the front of the violin body, but it's not known what techniques Stradivari and Guarneri used to treat the wood, which is what affects the violin's sound.

There are some theories about these techniques, however. One theory is that prolonged immersion in seawater made the wood more porous, thereby allowing the sound to vibrate freely. Another theory suggests that the tone was the result of the great attention paid to the reddish-brown varnish applied in the final stage of production. We know that each violin maker painstakingly guarded the method of the preparation and use of the varnish, which not only enhanced the **acoustical** properties of the instruments but also gave them a rich, beautiful **patina**.

Following the deaths of Stradivari and Guarneri and their immediate successors, violin making in Cremona became a lost art until 1938, when an attempt was made to **resuscitate** it. In that year, a school for violin makers was opened under the **auspices** of the Italian government. Enrollment is limited to one hundred, and only one applicant in four is accepted. On successfully completing the four-year course, students receive the coveted *maestro di liuteria* diploma.

The 700-year-old Cremona city hall houses a fine collection of violins, including a Stradivarius, a Guarnerius, and two Amatis. Every morning, a **rapt** audience of students from the school and visiting tourists listen to the **mellifluous** music as the **curator** of the instruments plays one or two of them to keep them in good form.

Answer each of the following questions in the form of a sentence. If a question does not contain a vocabulary word from this lesson's word list, use one in your answer. Use each word only once.

1. How did Stradivari learn his craft?

2. Who might **cavil** at the claim that Stradivari was the **nonpareil** of violin makers?

3. How does the passage suggest that the sound qualities of Stradivarius and Guarnerius violins are beyond words?

4. What's the difference between a Guarnerius and a Stradivarius violin?

5. What is a violin made of?

6. What gives these old violins their rich appearance?

7. Why was there a need to **resuscitate** violin making in Cremona in 1938?

8. Why might a violin player envy the instruments **curator** of the Cremona town hall?

9. How does the passage describe the audience that visits Cremona's city hall every morning?

10. What does the audience at the Cremona city hall listen to?

FUN & FASCINATING FACTS

Both the words **august** and the month of August were derived from the Latin word *augustus*, which means "most high." The name Augustus was awarded to Octavius Caesar, two years after he became the first Roman emperor in 29 B.C. The Romans also named a month after him. Incidentally, Augustus was the grand-nephew of Julius Caesar, after whom the month of July is named.

The Latin word for "honey" is *mel*. It combines with the Latin *fluus*, which means "flowing," to form **mellifluous**. A *mellifluous* sound is sweet to the ear and can be said to "flow like honey."

Lesson 19

Word List

Study the definitions of the words below; then do the exercises for the lesson.

amenable
ə men´ ə bəl

adj. Responsive; willing to be controlled or to take advice.
The director was **amenable** to our suggested changes in the schedule and implemented them promptly.

ascribe
ə skrīb´

v. To attribute to a source or a cause.
The Passionate Pilgrim is a collection of poems, some of which are **ascribed** to Shakespeare; the authorship of the others is unknown.

charisma
kə riz´ mə

n. A special quality in a person that inspires devotion or fascination in others.
Charisma is a definite asset if you're running for office.
charismatic *adj.* (kə riz mat´ ik)
Popular leaders tend to be highly **charismatic**.

dearth
dʉrth

n. Scarcity; a shortage.
There was a **dearth** of good restaurants around the waterfront until the city extended the subway there.

demoralize
dē môr´ ə līz

v. To destroy the morals or morale of someone; to weaken the spirit or courage of someone.
The band members were **demoralized** by the poor attendance at their final concert.

ebullient
e bul´ yənt

adj. Bubbling with enthusiasm or high spirits.
Ebullient fans, ecstatic over their team's victory, carried the captain of the team off the field in triumph.
ebullience *n.*
Ruth's natural **ebullience** always cheers me up when I feel low.

entrepreneur
än trə prə noor´

n. An individual who manages and takes the risk of a business.
The Small Business Administration gives loans and advice to **entrepreneurs** starting new businesses.
entrepreneurial *adj.*
Vanessa's **entrepreneurial** spirit became apparent when she organized an alternative to the school's lunch provider.

fatuous
fach´ ōō əs

adj. Foolish; silly; stupid.
Jenna was getting annoyed at Malcolm for the **fatuous** grin with which he greeted her every suggestion.

harbinger
här´ bin jər

n. A person or thing that is a symbol of what is to come.
According to American tradition, the appearance of a groundhog's shadow on February 2 is a **harbinger** of six more weeks of winter.

homogeneous
hō mō jē´ nē əs

adj. Of a similar kind or nature; uniform throughout.
The walking club was made up of a **homogeneous** group of middle-class, working mothers.
homogeneity *n.* (hō mō jə nē´ ə tē)
Too much **homogeneity** in the book group makes for a boring discussion.

incumbent in kum´ bənt	*n.* One who occupies an office or position. George Washington was the first **incumbent** of the U.S. presidency. *adj.* 1. Currently in office. The **incumbent** mayor has only been in office since her election last year. 2. (used with *on* or *upon*) Resting upon as a duty or obligation. It is **incumbent** upon the new office manager to improve the benefits package.
matriarchy mā´ trē är kē	*n.* A society that is headed by a female. African elephants live in a **matriarchy** that excludes males from the herd when they reach about five years old. **matriarchal** *adj.* Honeybees live in **matriarchal** colonies organized around a queen bee.
neophyte nē´ ə fīt	*n.* A beginner; a novice. Most students in the playwriting class were **neophytes** who had never written a play before.
prerogative prē räg´ ə tiv	*n.* A special right limited to a person, group, or office; a privilege. It is the governor's **prerogative** to pardon convicted felons.
sibling sib´ liŋ	*n.* One of two or more people who have the same parents; brother or sister. Sila had seven **siblings**: three sisters and four brothers.

19A Understanding Meanings

Read the sentences below. If a sentence correctly uses the word in bold, write *C* on the line below it. If a sentence is incorrect, rewrite it so that the vocabulary word in bold is used correctly.

1. A **matriarchy** is a group made up exclusively of females.

2. An **incumbent** is an elected official who is still serving in office.

3. A **prerogative** is an indication of what is to come in the future.

4. **Ebullience** is the inability to distinguish right from wrong.

5. To **demoralize** someone is to lecture that person on proper conduct.

6. **Charisma** is a quality that induces people to follow one who possesses it.

7. **Entrepreneurial** skills are those concerned with business ventures.

8. To **ascribe** blame to someone is to hold that person responsible.

9. A **neophyte** is an ephemeral event or thing.

10. A **dearth** of something is a shortage of it.

11. **Siblings** are one's brothers and sisters.

12. A **homogeneous** mixture is the same throughout.

13. An **amenable** person is one who is easily persuaded or dissuaded.

14. A **harbinger** is a species of bird.

15. A **fatuous** remark is one that is foolish.

amenable
ascribe
charisma
dearth
demoralize
ebullient
entrepreneur
fatuous
harbinger
homogeneous
incumbent
matriarchy
neophyte
prerogative
sibling

19B Using Words

If the word (or a form of the word) in bold fits in a sentence in the group below it, write the word in the blank. If the word does not fit, leave the space empty.

1. amenable

(a) The owner is _____ to our suggestion that we close the store for renovations.

(b) Helena expected an argument from her brother, but he proved _____ and helped her with the dishes without a protest.

(c) If this proposal is _____ to Jesse, he should sign it on the dotted line.

2. demoralized

(a) The students were _____ by the huge amount of homework that was assigned to them.

(b) The candidate was _____ after his crushing defeat at the polls.

(c) The lack of rain has _____ the corn and soybean crops.

3. fatuous

(a) It is _____ to claim that everyone can learn to play the guitar in three easy lessons.

(b) Lionel's cat had grown to be incredibly _____ so Lionel put her on a diet.

(c) _____ should be avoided because it can lead to high cholesterol and heart disease.

4. prerogative

(a) Before the abolition of slavery in the United States, freeing a slave was the _____ of the slave owner.

(b) A _____ sentence is one ending in a question mark.

(c) It was Sophia's _____ as president of the student council to schedule all council meetings.

5. ascribe

(a) Can you _____ what the man who robbed you looked like?

(b) To what do you _____ your success at school?

(c) Most scholars _____ this painting to Monet.

6. dearth

(a) A reduction in funding could easily mean the _____ of the project.

(b) The _____ of affordable housing in the city made me decide to move to a small town.

(c) The _____ of good soil around here makes it difficult to grow crops.

7. incumbent

(a) The political challenger usually finds it difficult to defeat the _____ .

(b) When I walked in, I found my dog lying in an _____ position on the sofa.

(c) It is _____ on me to help my little brother with his homework.

8. homogeneous

(a) There are few ethnic or racial divisions in Japan's _____ population.

(b) Flour and flower are _____ words.

(c) Lydia was so tired and _____ that she almost fell asleep during class.

19C Word Study

In the blank spaces, write the prefix *re-* ("again", "back") or *pre-* ("before", "forward") and the correct vocabulary word. The number in parentheses shows the lesson in which the word appears.

1. The prefix _____ combines with the Latin *menisci* (mind) to form the

   English word _____ , (8) "to think or talk about the past."

2. The prefix _____ combines with the Latin *cedere* (to go) to form the

   English word _____ , (15) "one who has gone before."

3. The prefix _____ combines with the Latin *diligere* (to love) to form the

   English word _____ , (16) "an inclination or preference."

4. The prefix _____ combines with the Latin *pascere* (to feed) to form the

   English word _____ , (6) "a meal; food and drink."

5. The prefix _____ combines with the Latin *surgere* (to rise) to form the

   English word _____ , (7) "a rising again to life."

6. The prefix _____ combines with the Latin *compensare* (to pay) to form the

   English word _____ , (6) "to pay."

7. The prefix _____ combines with the Latin *meditari* (to ponder) to form the

   English word _____ , (12) "planned beforehand."

8. The prefix _____ combines with the Latin *texere* (to weave) to form the

   English word _____ , (13) "an effort to conceal one's true intention."

amenable
ascribe
charisma
dearth
demoralize
ebullient
entrepreneur
fatuous
harbinger
homogeneous
incumbent
matriarchy
neophyte
prerogative
sibling

9. The prefix _____ combines with the Latin *parare* (to put in order) to form

the English word _____ , (3) "a making up for a wrong that was done."

10. The prefix _____ combines with the Latin *rogare* (to ask) to form the

English word _____ , (19) "a privilege or special right."

19D Images of Words

Circle the letter of each sentence that suggests the numbered bold vocabulary word. In each group, you may circle more than one letter or none at all.

1. **dearth**

    (a) The food tasted so bad we hardly touched it.

    (b) Damon's little sister was too short to be allowed onto the roller coaster at the amusement park.

    (c) Chris was on the waiting list to purchase a hybrid car.

2. **charisma**

    (a) High heels aren't considered as fashionable as they were twenty years ago.

    (b) The Jeep was one of the best-selling vehicles of recent years.

    (c) The leader of the group inspired extraordinary loyalty in her followers.

3. **harbinger**

    (a) As the dark clouds rolled in, it became obvious that a storm was approaching.

    (b) The bell rang every hour, on the hour.

    (c) The crocuses peeping through the ground meant that spring was coming.

4. **matriarchy**

    (a) The hospital's new wing is for women giving birth.

    (b) A mother's love for her child is captured in this series of photographs.

    (c) The queen ruled until her death, at which time her daughter became monarch.

5. **ebullience**

    (a) The life jacket is designed to keep people afloat in water.

    (b) Kenya was so excited about her upcoming vacation that she was beaming with delight.

    (c) Terry was so thrilled to get the part in the school play that he couldn't contain himself.

6. **entrepreneur**

    (a) Corinne started up and ran a clothing store that sold a lot of her own designs.

    (b) Monica's catering business is doing really well.

    (c) For most of his working life, Jeremy was a senior manager with a major insurance company.

7. **sibling**

(a) The colt was just a few minutes old and still wobbly on its feet.

(b) Beth has a younger brother and an older sister.

(c) Jorge and his cousin Anton were best friends.

8. **prerogative**

(a) In 1920, women had the right to vote in the United States for the first time.

(b) The president of the United States has the right to veto legislation proposed by Congress.

(c) Newtonian physics dictates that for every action, there's an equal and opposite reaction.

9. **demoralize**

(a) Our basketball team was dejected after losing nine games in a row.

(b) It's disturbing how Jolene has no compunction about being rude to others.

(c) When Patrick's business didn't make money right away, he was ready to quit altogether.

10. **neophyte**

(a) Her friends smiled when they saw Shay holding the chopsticks by the wrong end.

(b) It's natural to be scared when you make your first parachute jump.

(c) Remove the protective seal from the grill before using it for the first time.

19E Passage

Read the passage below; then complete the exercise that follows it.

Wilma Mankiller, Chief of the Cherokee

amenable
ascribe
charisma
dearth
demoralize
ebullient
entrepreneur
fatuous
harbinger
homogeneous
incumbent
matriarchy
neophyte
prerogative
sibling

In 1985, Wilma Mankiller became the first female principal chief of the Cherokee Nation, the second largest Native American tribe, with a population of 108,000. Her rise to power appears to be a **harbinger** of change in a largely male-dominated society, even though, in times past, Cherokee society had been a **matriarchy** in which important decisions such as whether or not to go to war had been the **prerogative** of the women of the tribe.

Although as a trained social worker she had been active in community affairs, Mankiller was a political **neophyte** when she ran for the office of deputy chief in 1983. She was the running mate of principal chief Ross Swimmer, who was impressed by her **charismatic** leadership of a community revitalization project in which the residents of a poverty-stricken community worked together to build and renovate housing and water systems. This project was compatible with Mankiller's belief that Native Americans benefit from solving their own problems instead of relying on help from outside the community.

Ross Swimmer and Mankiller won the election in which they ran together. Two years later, when Swimmer resigned in order to head the Bureau of Indian Affairs, Mankiller took his place. As tribal leader, Mankiller oversaw an operation that runs a number of businesses in the manufacturing, ranching, and tourism industries. For a second term in 1987, Mankiller ran as an **incumbent**, winning with 56 percent of the vote. She **ascribed** her victory to her tireless efforts to improve employment opportunities, education, housing, and health facilities for her tribe.

Mankiller's philosophy of government calls for Cherokee self-reliance. She encourages an **entrepreneurial** spirit among the Cherokee instead of looking to Washington for economic support, which she believes can have a **demoralizing** effect on Native Americans. As she states in her autobiography, *Mankiller: A Chief and Her People*, "I . . . want to be remembered for emphasizing the fact that we have indigenous solutions to our problems." Native Americans are not a **homogenous** people. In Mankiller's book she writes of a lack of strong Native American leaders, partly as a result of the diversity of cultures and languages. Great past leaders like Sioux chief Sitting Bull and Apache chief Geronimo had influence only over their own tribes.

Mankiller's **ebullient** spirit has frequently been tested by health problems. In 1979, she underwent several operations after she was nearly killed in a head-on car collision that did kill a close friend. Shortly afterward, she learned that she had muscular dystrophy. Fortunately, the disease proved **amenable** to surgery and drug treatment. Then in 1990, kidney failure brought her close to death again. Her **siblings** (Mankiller is one of eleven children) were tested as possible kidney donors, and her brother Don provided the closest match. In a successful three-hour operation, one of Don's healthy kidneys was removed and given to Mankiller. But she believes that facing death and overcoming her health problems has made her more courageous and able to become a better leader: "I realized I could survive anything. I had faced adversity and turned it into a positive experience—a better path." When she ran for a third term in 1991, Mankiller's opponent tried to make her health an issue, but with little success. She received an impressive 83 percent of the vote. She decided not to run for a fourth term in 1995, however.

Wilma Mankiller is proud to be called an ardent feminist. In 1987, she was named "Woman of the Year" by *Ms.* magazine, and in 1993 she was inducted into the National Women's Hall of Fame. She has expressed concerns about the **dearth** of female Cherokee leaders, and by her own success has provided an example for others to follow. In a **fatuous** editorial, one newspaper writer suggested a link between her name and her feminist politics. In fact, the name Mankiller originally was a military rank applied to one who guarded the tribe. Wilma Mankiller likes this association; she is proud of her surname.

Answer each of the following questions in the form of a sentence. If a question does not contain a vocabulary word from this lesson's word list, use one in your answer. Use each word only once.

1. In what sense was the Cherokee nation once a **matriarchal** society?

2. What reason would there be for voting against Mankiller when she was running for the office of deputy chief?

3. What does it mean to say that Mankiller ran as an **incumbent** in 1987?

4. To what could one **ascribe** Mankiller's success as a leader?

5. Why did Mankiller try to promote an **entrepreneurial** spirit among her people?

6. What quality of Wilma Mankiller's helped her overcome both illness and political opposition?

7. Is there any evidence that Mankiller has **charisma**?

8. Why is the editorial that pokes fun at Mankiller's name described as **fatuous**?

9. What concern has Mankiller expressed about women in the Cherokee nation?

10. What must transpire for Mankiller's election to be a **harbinger** of change for women leaders?

FUN & FASCINATING FACTS

The Old English word *deorthu* had two meanings: it meant both "sparse" and "expensive." Eventually, each meaning got its own word from *deorthu*: **dearth** and *dear*.

Herberge* is an Old Germanic word for "shelter." In medieval times, when travel was difficult and laborious, sometimes a person was sent ahead of a group to arrange lodgings at an inn. This person, who made innkeepers aware that travelers were coming, was called a *herbengar*. Eventually the word **harbinger** came to mean any sign of things to come.

The Greek *homo-*, "same," and *genos*, "kind," combine to form **homogeneous**. A number of other English words share this prefix. *Homogenized* milk has had the fat broken down so that the cream and milk are no longer separated and the resulting liquid all looks the same. *Homonyms* are words that sound the same but which have different meanings and usually different spellings. *Homographs* are words that have the same spelling but different meanings. (The *Polish* man had to *polish* his shoes for the party.)

The Latin word *mater*, meaning "mother," and the Greek *arkhein*, meaning "rule," combine to form **matriarchy**. Several other words are formed from this Greek root. A *monarchy* is rule by a single king or queen. An *oligarchy* is rule by a few, usually members of several powerful families. A *hierarchy* (Lesson 1) is a system of rule in which there are higher and lower positions of power.

Lesson 20

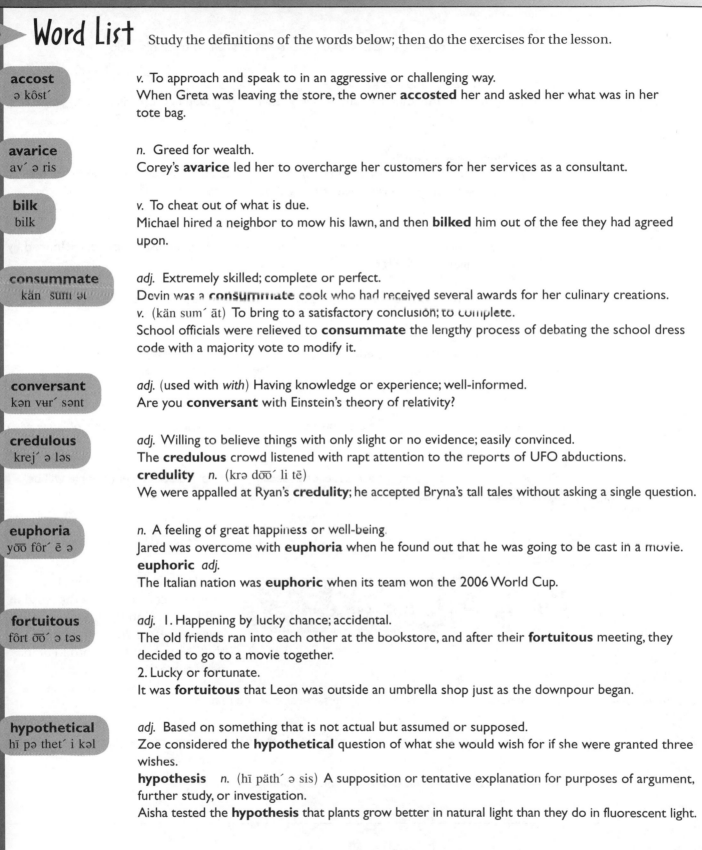

> ## Word List
Study the definitions of the words below; then do the exercises for the lesson.

accost
ə kôst´

v. To approach and speak to in an aggressive or challenging way.
When Greta was leaving the store, the owner **accosted** her and asked her what was in her tote bag.

avarice
av´ ə ris

n. Greed for wealth.
Corey's **avarice** led her to overcharge her customers for her services as a consultant.

bilk
bilk

v. To cheat out of what is due.
Michael hired a neighbor to mow his lawn, and then **bilked** him out of the fee they had agreed upon.

consummate
kän´ sum ət

adj. Extremely skilled; complete or perfect.
Devin was a **consummate** cook who had received several awards for her culinary creations.
v. (kän sum´ āt) To bring to a satisfactory conclusion; to complete.
School officials were relieved to **consummate** the lengthy process of debating the school dress code with a majority vote to modify it.

conversant
kən vur´ sənt

adj. (used with *with*) Having knowledge or experience; well-informed.
Are you **conversant** with Einstein's theory of relativity?

credulous
krej´ ə ləs

adj. Willing to believe things with only slight or no evidence; easily convinced.
The **credulous** crowd listened with rapt attention to the reports of UFO abductions.
credulity *n.* (krə dōo´ li tē)
We were appalled at Ryan's **credulity**; he accepted Bryna's tall tales without asking a single question.

euphoria
yōo fôr´ ē ə

n. A feeling of great happiness or well-being.
Jared was overcome with **euphoria** when he found out that he was going to be cast in a movie.
euphoric *adj.*
The Italian nation was **euphoric** when its team won the 2006 World Cup.

fortuitous
fôrt ōo´ ə təs

adj. 1. Happening by lucky chance; accidental.
The old friends ran into each other at the bookstore, and after their **fortuitous** meeting, they decided to go to a movie together.
2. Lucky or fortunate.
It was **fortuitous** that Leon was outside an umbrella shop just as the downpour began.

hypothetical
hī pə thet´ i kəl

adj. Based on something that is not actual but assumed or supposed.
Zoe considered the **hypothetical** question of what she would wish for if she were granted three wishes.
hypothesis *n.* (hī päth´ ə sis) A supposition or tentative explanation for purposes of argument, further study, or investigation.
Aisha tested the **hypothesis** that plants grow better in natural light than they do in fluorescent light.

incoherent
in kō hir´ ənt

adj. Not connected; confused; rambling.
Because the lecturer had no time to prepare for her talk, she delivered an **incoherent** speech that was hard to follow.
incoherence *n.*
Because of the **incoherence** of Carl's argument, it was difficult to trace his logic.

minuscule
mi´ nus kyōōl

adj. Very small in size or importance.
Tyrone added just a **minuscule** amount of chili pepper to the soup because his mother doesn't like it when it's too spicy.

pleasantry
plez´ ən trē

n. An agreeable, casual remark.
Whitney and Yvette didn't know each other very well, so when they ran into each other on the street, they would simply exchange **pleasantries** about their families and the weather.

procrastinate
prō kras´ ti nāt

v. To put off until later.
Instead of starting her homework as soon as she came home, Meredith usually **procrastinated** by watching TV or calling friends first.
procrastination *n.*
Because of Ian's **procrastination**, the tickets to the concert were sold out by the time he called to order them.

qualm
kwäm

n. A feeling of uneasiness as to whether what one is doing is right or wise; a misgiving.
Noah had **qualms** about accepting money for shopping for his elderly neighbor.

stigma
stig´ mə

n. A mark of shame or disgrace.
After she was caught cheating on the Spanish test, Sasha had to deal with the **stigma** of being seen as dishonest.
stigmatize *v.* To give a bad name to.
Some people object to publicizing arrest records because they fear that innocent people will be **stigmatized**.

accost
avarice
bilk
consummate
conversant
credulous
euphoria
fortuitous
hypothetical
incoherent
minuscule
pleasantry
procrastinate
qualm
stigma

20A Understanding Meanings

Read the sentences below. If a sentence correctly uses the word in bold, write *C* on the line below it. If a sentence is incorrect, rewrite it so that the vocabulary word in bold is used correctly.

1. A **minuscule** portion is one that is the same size as the rest.

2. **Euphoria** is mercy shown to a vulnerable opponent.

3. To **accost** someone is to confront that person in a hostile manner.

4. A **qualm** is a twinge of uncertainty.

5. **Avarice** is an excessive desire for wealth.

6. An **incoherent** speech is one that is disjointed and wandering.

7. To be **conversant** with a subject is to be familiar with it.

8. A **hypothesis** is a conjecture.

9. To **stigmatize** someone is to reward that person.

10. A **pleasantry** is a tasty morsel of food.

11. **Credulity** is a willingness to believe without evidence.

12. A **fortuitous** incident is one that is invented or made up.

13. A **consummate** musician is one of very great skill.

14. **Procrastination** is delaying a task or activity until later.

15. To **bilk** someone is to swindle that person.

20B Using Words

If the word (or a form of the word) in bold fits in a sentence in the group below it, write the word in the blank. If the word does not fit, leave the space empty.

1. **bilk**

 (a) They were able to _____ the phone company by putting the account in a false name.

 (b) The pony _____ at jumping the hedge and swerved away at the last second.

 (c) To avoid being _____ , don't pay for the repairs until they are completed.

2. **fortuitous**

 (a) I was feeling _____ , so I decided to spend a dollar on a lottery ticket.

 (b) A _____ combination of circumstances led paleontologists to discover the buried dinosaur fossils.

 (c) It was _____ that Emile bought a shovel the day before the snowstorm.

3. **incoherent**

 (a) The speaker launched into an _____ outburst that we could not understand.

 (b) Ken considered the _____ effects of the aftermath of the storm.

 (c) A single blow of the sledgehammer reduced the boulder to _____ fragments.

4. **accost**

 (a) Two police officers _____ the man with the package as he left the building.

 (b) The restaurant host _____ us with a friendly smile and led us to a table.

 (c) The man timidly _____ us and asked for directions to the ballpark.

5. **conversant**

 (a) I can read Spanish but I'm not a good _____ in the language.

 (b) Are you _____ with the theory that a meteorite led to the extinction of dinosaurs?

 (c) Many people in seventeenth-century Italy believed that the sun revolved around the earth, but Galileo argued that the _____ was true.

6. **consummate**

 (a) Anna is a _____ artist and is considered to be a nonpareil in her field.

 (b) It took him less than ten minutes to _____ the *New York Times* crossword puzzle.

 (c) At the end of the long meeting, the two parties finally _____ the deal.

accost
avarice
bilk
consummate
conversant
credulous
euphoria
fortuitous
hypothetical
incoherent
minuscule
pleasantry
procrastinate
qualm
stigma

7. **credulous**

    (a) The library received _____ reports that the missing books had been found.

    (b) Sara must be pretty _____ to believe such a ridiculous story.

    (c) The staff made a _____ effort to put out the newsletter on time.

8. **hypothetical**

    (a) Consider a _____ situation in which you could travel through time.

    (b) To make false promises is _____ to everything Willa believes in.

    (c) Some scientists are willing to entertain the _____ notion that life exists on other planets.

20C Word Study

Complete the analogies by selecting the pair of words whose relationship most resembles the relationship of the pair in capital letters. Circle the letter in front of the pair you choose.

1. HOMILY : INSTRUCT ::
    (a) accolade : condone   (c) conundrum : baffle
    (b) obituary : amuse   (d) manifesto : reward

2. MELLIFLUOUS : SOUND ::
    (a) attractive : infatuation   (c) delicious : taste
    (b) volatile : temperament   (d) decrepit : condition

3. ACOUSTIC : SOUND ::
    (a) olfactory : smell   (c) onerous : task
    (b) doleful : misery   (d) rusty : patina

4. SIBLING : SISTER ::
    (a) matriarchy : female   (c) posterity : descendant
    (b) confidant : friend   (d) parent : mother

5. NEOPHYTE : INEXPERIENCED ::
    (a) luminary : baleful   (c) introvert : shy
    (b) visionary : unaware   (d) gourmet : esoteric

6. DEMORALIZE : REJUVENATE ::
    (a) instigate : expedite   (c) mesmerize : denigrate
    (b) exacerbate : ameliorate   (d) liquidate : proselytize

7. AVARICE : WEALTH ::
    (a) ambivalence : doubt   (c) vanity : beauty
    (b) compunction : pity   (d) acrimony : discard

8. HAPPINESS : EUPHORIA ::

   (a) decorum : prosperity   (c) behavior : decorum

   (b) asperity : vestige   (d) dislike : enmity

9. INCOHERENT : LUCID ::

   (a) muddled : clear   (c) adamant : circuitous

   (b) antiquated : spurious   (d) cloudy : celestial

10. INIQUITOUS : INNOCUOUS ::

   (a) onerous : omnivorous   (c) plebeian : perverse

   (b) baleful : laudatory   (d) scathing : scurrilous

20D Images of Words

Circle the letter of each sentence that suggests the numbered bold vocabulary word. In each group, you may circle more than one letter or none at all.

1. **avarice**

   (a) Maurice loved money more than anything else.

   (b) Belinda was desperate to win the chess game.

   (c) Jocelyn took a job at an investment firm with the sole goal of making a lot of money.

2. **incoherence**

   (a) In his dazed state, what Jim said made little sense.

   (b) The ship broke apart when it ran aground on the rocky coast.

   (c) The parts of the model airplane came apart soon after it was assembled.

3. **stigma**

   (a) No one believed Bruce because he was a known liar.

   (b) When Alicia turned two, she suddenly began having temper tantrums.

   (c) Whenever Gabe appeared in town, people murmured about his cowardice when his family's house caught on fire.

4. **hypothesis**

   (a) When it's noon in New York, it is 9 a.m. in California.

   (b) If you go out in the rain, bring an umbrella.

   (c) Some scholars believe that humans are born with a predisposition to learn a language.

5. **fortuitous**

   (a) By chance, Henry ran into an acquaintance he hadn't seen in ages, who offered him a great job.

   (b) It happens that my friend and I were born on the same day.

   (c) They were just giving up hope of finding their cat when she returned home on her own.

accost
avarice
bilk
consummate
conversant
credulous
euphoria
fortuitous
hypothetical
incoherent
minuscule
pleasantry
procrastinate
qualm
stigma

6. **pleasantry**

    (a) Three friends spent the afternoon drifting down the gently flowing stream on a raft.

    (b) Robert said how well Juan looked and asked about his parents and sister.

    (c) Celia was relieved to hear the words, "You're hired!"

7. **euphoria**

    (a) Fear of falling kept me from getting too close to the edge of the cliff.

    (b) Fans celebrated through the night when the Rangers won the Stanley Cup.

    (c) Crystal refuses to fly so she takes the train instead.

8. **procrastinate**

    (a) The paper was due in two days, and Glen still hadn't thought of a topic.

    (b) Carla meant to write a thank-you letter promptly, but didn't get around to it for over a month.

    (c) Everyone was stunned at how rude Sharon was being.

9. **minuscule**

    (a) Anyone would need a magnifying glass to read that writing.

    (b) Two hundred and fifty million atoms laid side by side measure about one inch.

    (c) We had less than one-tenth of an inch of rain last month.

10. **qualm**

    (a) Khalil got into a minor argument with his brother.

    (b) Lyle felt terrible about refusing to help, but he really had no choice.

    (c) The sharp pain in Shawna's ankle made her think that she had sprained it.

20E Passage

Read the passage below; then complete the exercise that follows it.

Too Good to Be True

Consider the following **hypothetical** situation: You are a struggling New York actor hoping for a break. When you are almost ready to quit, your phone rings. The caller identifies himself as the casting director for a well-known film company. After you exchange a few **pleasantries**, he offers you a small speaking part in a major motion picture. You're **euphoric** at first, but then the caller asks if you are a member of the Screen Actors Guild (SAG), a necessary condition for employment. You admit that you are not.

At this point, you expect the conversation to end, but the caller suggests that you take out a temporary SAG membership. The cost is only five hundred dollars, really a **minuscule** amount compared to how much you'll be making from the movie. You can't afford the membership fee, but you can't afford to **procrastinate** either, since filming will start in a matter of days. He urges you to get the ball rolling by wiring the money to an address he gives you. Would you agree to do it? Not if you were thinking clearly.

Every year, millions of Americans are **bilked** by con artists. They are robbed as surely as if they had been held up, except that the con artists' weapon is their ability to persuade their victims to take advantage of opportunities that seem too good to miss. Without a **qualm**, they will steal a retired couple's life savings or an aspiring actor's last five hundred dollars. A milder **stigma** is attached to these con artists than to their fellow criminals who use cruder, more physical means, although like muggers and burglars, they, too, are motivated by **avarice**.

A possible reason why so many people become victims of con artists is that most of us are not sufficiently informed about how con artists work or how to detect a swindle. That is why the following information is very important.

In order to be successful, con artists can't be **incoherent** and inarticulate; they must be **consummate** liars, well practiced and smooth. In addition, they should be **conversant** with their victim's circumstances and weaknesses, knowing whether the person is desperate or greedy, and how **credulous** he or she is. Con artists also must have the ability to establish a quick rapport with the victim, who is commonly referred to in the trade as "the mark," "the chump," "the sucker," or "the egg."

Scams take many forms: victims are bombarded over the phone, through the mail, over the Internet, via television and newspaper ads, and in person. Often victims are **accosted** by persuasive, fast-talking con artists, who convince them that if they act immediately, they will be able to take advantage of a **fortuitous** opportunity that has fallen into their lap. Generally, con artists prey on the universal hopes for fortune, success, and good health. They ask for immediate cash or information, such as your credit card or Social Security number, in exchange for promises of millions in prize money, a free vacation, an inviting career opportunity, or a miracle cure.

Anyone can reduce her or his chances of being the victim of a con artist by following these tips: never give out information over the phone; be wary of situations in which you're pressed to make on-the-spot decisions or pay for something immediately; and avoid making secret deals. Victims of con artists can save themselves a lot of grief if they remember the aphorism, "If it sounds too good to be true, it probably is."

Answer each of the following questions in the form of a sentence. If a question does not contain a vocabulary word from this lesson's word list, use one in your answer. Use each word only once.

1. Why is the story of the struggling actor described as **hypothetical**?

2. Why would a con artist begin a conversation with a few **pleasantries**?

accost
avarice
bilk
consummate
conversant
credulous
euphoria
fortuitous
hypothetical
incoherent
minuscule
pleasantry
procrastinate
qualm
stigma

3. Why would con artists discourage their victims from **procrastinating**?

4. Are many Americans cheated by con artists?

5. What sentence in the passage indicates that con artists do not have any guilt or misgivings about stealing other people's money?

6. What human trait do con artists and their victims sometimes share?

7. What ability must con artists possess if they want to be successful?

8. Why would it be helpful for con artists to be **conversant** with the circumstances of the person they are cheating?

9. Do you think it is likely that a stranger could convince you to take advantage of a **fortuitous** opportunity?

10. Why do you think victims of con artists might be reluctant to report the crime?

FUN & FASCINATING FACTS

The Latin *credere* means "to believe." It forms the root of several English words. If one puts *credence* in a statement, one is willing to believe it. A *credible* witness is one whose testimony can be believed. A *credo* is a formal statement of one's beliefs. And a **credulous** person is someone who is willing to believe without proof and is therefore easily deceived.

The Greek prefix *eu-* means "good" or "well" and is found in several English words. A *euphemism* (Lesson 6) is a mild, less offensive term for one that is harsh or negative. A *eulogy* is a speech delivered on someone's death in which one says only good things about that person. A *euphonious* sound is one that is pleasing to the ear. And *euphoria* is a feeling of great well-being.

Review for Lessons 17–20

Crossword Puzzle Solve the crossword puzzle below by studying the clues and filling in the answer boxes. Clues followed by a number are definitions of words in Lessons 17 through 20. The number gives the word list in which the answer to the clue appears.

Clues Across

1. Scarcity; a shortage (19)

4. Possessing qualities that inspire devotion (19)

10. A feeling of uneasiness or misgiving (20)

11. A casual, agreeable remark (20)

12. A person's manner (18)

14. Worn on the feet

16. A brother or sister (19)

17. A fortified area or position (17)

19. Synonym for *mad*

21. River that runs through Egypt

22. Between *rare* and *well done*

23. A kind of wood that lines closets or chests

24. Silly or stupid (19)

26. A feeling of great happiness (20)

27. Inspiring great respect or admiration (18)

28. Pleasant to the ear (18)

Clues Down

2. Bubbling with enthusiasm (19)

3. Reckless boldness (17)

5. Great exaggeration (17)

6. To plead for in a pestering way (17)

7. Western state

8. Capital of France

9. Uniform throughout (19)

13. A person or thing without equal (18)

15. Easily convinced (20)

18. To think over (17)

20. Fully absorbed; engrossed (18)

23. To criticize unimportant things (18)

24. Abbreviation for "influenza"

25. "_____ and downs"